HE HAS BROUGHT ME LOW SO I CAN SOAR

JOY HANEY

HE HAS BROUGHT ME LOW SO I CAN SOAR

WORD AFLAME PRESS
WELDON SPRING, MO

Word Aflame Press
36 Research Park Court
Weldon Spring, MO 63304
pentecostalpublishing.com

All Scripture verses quoted are from the King James Version unless otherwise identified.

Scripture verses marked (NKJV) from the New King James Version © 1982 by Thomas Nelson, Inc.; (NIV) from the New International Version © 1973, 1978, 1984, 2011 by Biblica, Inc.™ www.zondervan.com; (NLT) from the New Living Translation © 1996, 2004, 2015 by Tyndale House Foundation. Used by permission. All rights reserved.

A portion of chapter 7 is from *The Blessing of the Prison* © 1995 by Radiant Life. Used by permission. All rights reserved.

A portion of chapter 10 is from *The Anointed Ones* by Kenneth Haney © 1992 by Radiant Life. Used by permission. All rights reserved.

Printed in the United States of America

Cover design by Elizabeth Loyd

Library of Congress Cataloging-in-Publication Data

Names: Haney, Joy, 1942- author.
Title: He has brought me low so I can soar / Joy Haney.
Description: Weldon Spring : Word Aflame Press, 2018. | Includes bibliographical references. |
Identifiers: LCCN 2018038207 (print) | LCCN 2018038537 (ebook) | ISBN 9780757751691 | ISBN 9780757751684 (alk. paper)
Subjects: LCSH: Suffering--Religious aspects--Christianity.
Classification: LCC BV4909 (ebook) | LCC BV4909 .H3625 2018 (print) | DDC 248.8/6--dc23
LC record available at https://lccn.loc.gov/2018038207

Hannah prayed: "The Lord maketh poor, and maketh rich: he bringeth low, and lifteth up" (I Samuel 2:7).

Jeremiah lamented: "I am the man that hath seen affliction by the rod of his wrath. He hath led me, and brought me into darkness. . . . He hath hedged me about, that I cannot get out: he hath made my chain heavy" (Lamentations 3:1–2, 7).

The psalmist despaired: "You have laid me in the lowest pit, in darkness, in the depths" (Psalm 88:6, NKJV).

God saved: "I was brought low, and He saved me" (Psalm 116:6, NKJV).

CONTENTS

FOREWORD

If Joy Haney has ever been your friend, she is your friend still for she creates and maintains lifelong friendships. She is a woman of the Spirit and prayer and the Word — a devoted Christian. Her walk with God has taken her through dark valleys and led her to mountain peaks. Jesus Christ has, time and again, proven Himself faithful and true to her. Consequently, she has been faithful and true to Him.

There are not many writers whose published works number sixty-two. Over the years of her life and ministry, she has learned well the fine art of writing for the purpose of helping others, writing from her heart, writing with the heart and mind of God as her guide. With skill she weaves an unmistakable story of faith and trust while sharing her personal life experiences and citing the similarities between her life and ours — between our lives and those of men and women in the Word. Using poems, songs, Scripture verses, Bible stories, and her own life events, our dear friend, Joy Haney, once again takes the opportunity to remind us that regardless of how low we are brought, He calls us to soar!

Anthony & Mickey Mangun
Senior Pastor
The Pentecostals of Alexandria

Joy Haney is truly a woman of the Spirit. She is a godly woman. Early in her life she committed to furthering the cause of Christ, and her life has powerfully influenced the church world. She has the unique ability to identify very real needs in the body of Christ, expertly put pen to paper, and address those needs in a way that brings inspiration, edification, instruction, and revelation. *He Has Brought Me Low, so I Can Soar!* is her sixty-second book. In it she takes a candid look at a subject she has experienced firsthand—the pain, suffering, and tragedy associated with life and ministry and the way God raises a believer from the ashes of heartache and loss to a place of victory, anointing, and power.

We have had the privilege to know Bishop Kenneth Haney, First Lady Joy Haney, and their wonderful family most of our ministry. This powerful Apostolic couple influenced our lives, challenged our faith, and lifted our vision. Our testimony is not unique; countless ministers and believers around the world have been similarly affected. Their unwavering faith and faithfulness have brought a great blessing and example to all who have come in contact with them. Their anointed preaching, teaching, and writing have given inspiration and instruction to believers around the world. We will forever be thankful for the impact of their holy lifestyle, uplifting vision, and godly wisdom. They are a real dynamic duo.

November 10, 2011, was the beginning of the lowest and most difficult season of Joy Haney's life. On that day God called home her beloved husband, Bishop Haney. She enjoyed a half century of partnership in marriage, family, and ministry with the love of her life. God blessed their union with five wonderful children and twelve grand-children. They ministered side by side all the years of their marriage. Their unique talents and abilities created a winning partnership. They walked in harmony as best friends, allies, confidants, and colaborers in the vineyard of the Master. As powerful as they were together, one might surmise that when one was taken, the other would give up on ministry. Not so! It was the most painful loss of her life—the lowest point of her life—but she didn't give up. Instead she got back up and soared like an eagle.

Joy Haney's life experience makes *He Has Brought Me Low, so I Can Soar!* such a powerful book. Her life has been blessed. She has traveled the world. She copastored one of the largest Apostolic churches in North America. She was first lady of the largest Apostolic fellowship on earth. Perhaps most important, she is an overcomer and a survivor. No matter the pain and suffering and loss of life, she remained an overcomer. No matter what the evil spiritual forces of Hell waged against her, she was victorious. Joy Haney is a spiritual warrior. She understands and walks in the power of the Holy Spirit. She is a woman of prayer—she doesn't just talk and write about prayer; she is a woman of prayer. I am convinced that God and His angels, as well as the devil and his imps, are fully aware of the power this woman wields through prayer and faith.

In this book you will understand the power of never giving up. This book is a revelation of the power gained through holding to one's faith in times of adversity, loss, and seemingly insurmountable odds. No matter what you are going through—no matter who or what has come against you—this book will help you understand a life-changing principle understood by those who have battled and won in spiritual warfare—*He Has Brought Me Low, so I Can Soar!* Her years of faithful service to the Lord have taught her how to soar above the battle. She learned years ago how to commune with God, who is the greatest power of the universe. Because of the many years spent developing a strong relationship with God, she knows, no matter what life throws at her, human or spiritual, God will bring her to the other side of the battle soaring like an eagle.

Joy Haney serves as a powerful example of faith, fortitude, and fearlessness. We desire that the spirit of this wonderful woman of God will fall upon you. May the faith she possesses somehow take root in your life. Just as the hand of God is mightily upon her, we pray that as you internalize the words of this book, that same mighty hand of God will rest heavily upon you.

Jack & Elsy Cunningham
District Superintendent
Virginia District
United Pentecostal Church International

ACKNOWLEDGMENTS

A written manuscript becomes a published book with the help of many people. This book began with a word from God in 2014. It was spoken during a season of blessing but wasn't completed until four years later. Many things transpired in those four years, but the last two were what made it possible for me to write this book!

After the book was completed in its rough form, it first went to my long-time friend, a trusted editor, Bethany Sledge, who was in Germany doing missionary work with her husband. Under her skilled hand, she removed the rough edges and made it flow better. I thank her.

That copy then went to our long-time, round-the-world minister friends, Jack and Elsy Cunningham, so they could write a foreword for the book. They wrote a masterpiece, for which I am very thankful!

The copy also went to our worldwide minister friends, the illustrious and talented Anthony and Mickey Mangun. I am honored that they wrote an introductory foreword. I thank them.

My relationship with Pentecostal Publishing House and Word Aflame Press began in 1986. They have published nine of my books. It was my privilege to work with such capable Christian men such as J. O. Wallace, Marvin Curry, Robert Fuller, and others. They have always been fair and wonderful to work with, so I felt impressed to submit this manuscript to them.

That's where the book went next, but this time, there was a new editor in the Division of Publications: Everett Gossard. I met him through email, and when we talked on the phone, there was a bond. It was a bond shared by those who suffer. I was impressed with his work when he sent me a sample of his edits. Now, several months later, I can say he is thorough, articulate, and does excellent work! Special thanks to him for all his hard work and keen insight!

The first thing he did was meet with the Executive Publication Committee. I was honored to have the following great people decide the fate of my manuscript:

- Robin Johnston, editor in chief
- P. D. Buford, associate editor
- Lee Ann Alexander, associate editor
- Mark Blackburn, PPH administrator
- Jerry Jones, general secretary

I thank each one of them for all their hard work, and am thankful they agreed to publish this book, so that many people can see Jesus and His kingdom in a greater light when going through times of testing and trial.

The artwork for the book was then assigned to the talented cover designer, Elizabeth Loyd, who created the beautiful cover. When my daughter Angela saw it, she said it was "gloriously stunning!" When I sent it to Mickey Mangun, she echoed that sentiment, "Stunning!" Thank you, Elizabeth.

Special thanks also to the following people who were valuable in publishing this book; without them there would be no book:

- Tim Cummings, interior layout
- Melanie Loyd, proofreader
- Abraham LaVoi, marketing director
- Larry Craig, production manager

Lastly, I want to say a heartfelt thank you to Christian Life Center for their faithful, continued prayers for me, and also all the people in different parts of the country who prayed for me during my health crisis, and a special thank you to Josh Herring, whom God placed in my life during this time. Without prayer, you fight things alone, but with God, He fights for you, and He can do the impossible. Wonderful things happen when people pray!

I also want to thank all my family (especially my dear, precious children) for their faithful prayers, their tender, loving care for me, and making sure all my needs were met! Their Dad would have been proud of them!

Most of all, I want to be careful to give God all the glory! It was God that spoke the book into being. And He helped me write it. He allowed me to experience what it meant to be brought low, so I could better understand what He wanted me to write about. The purpose was bigger than the pain of the trial!

I am forever grateful to Him!

—Joy Haney

INTRODUCTION

In 2014 God spoke to me and gave me a title for a book. At the time I didn't totally understand it, but I started a file and worked on it a little. It didn't flow like some of the books He has impressed me to write, so I let it rest for a while, knowing He would bring to light exactly what He wanted in His time. Meanwhile, God inspired me to finish two other books I had been working on. After those were finished and published in 2015, He put a "fire" in me about another little handbook entitled *Baptism Is Essential!* He anointed me to find information, including historical facts, dealing with the original mode of baptism in Jesus' name and to put it all together. The book was printed, and everything seemed fine. Then I found out that the wonderful printing company we used to print the book had made some significant mistakes (which was unusual for them). I was heartsick and immediately called the company to explain the problem.

The president of the company called me back and was so kind. He said they would make it right, and they did. But much work was involved in the process, and I felt like I was being fought. I prayed for God to help us, and He did! It was a stressful time, but finally in January 2016 we received the new baptism handbooks, which were eagerly received by many.

Then on January 30, 2016, I became very sick, and my daughter took me to the hospital emergency room. They released me, but the sickness went on for a month with deep chest coughs, extreme weakness, earache, and other symptoms. During this time, again I heard the voice of the Lord, saying, "He has brought me low!" I was too sick to write anything but not too sick to listen. He kept bringing me thoughts, and I would mull them over and weep at His presence and His wisdom.

A little over a month later, another unfortunate thing occurred. A huge weeping willow tree cracked in half and fell onto my fence, causing much damage. We couldn't get in or out of our yard and had to call a man to cut branches that were blocking our entering or leaving! Getting bids to remove the tree from our damaged fence was stressful. Resolving this problem took another whole month, but finally in April it was completed. I was just thankful the tree hadn't fallen on our house!

PART OF MY FACE AND LEFT HAND WERE GOING NUMB.

But I felt like I was being fought and told my son, "I'm feeling a little like Job. In all my years of writing and publishing, this has never happened with any other book. And now this huge tree falling and causing so much damage, it just isn't normal!"

Less than a month later, on Friday, May 6, 2016, I was packed and getting ready to speak at another church on Sunday for Mother's Day. While talking on the phone, I felt something strange happening to me. Part of my face and left hand were going numb. I thought I'd walk it off. I went downstairs and started walking, but that didn't help. It scared me, so I called to Angela, our youngest daughter, and she heard the fear in my voice and ran downstairs. She helped me into the back bedroom, and we both started praying and calling on God. She also gave me some natural supplements, and finally there was relief!

It happened again one hour later, and when it happened the third time, I told Angela to call the kids and have them pray. Some of them rushed right over, and we agreed to call 911.

I have to tell you how traumatic this was for me. In all my life, I had never been admitted to a hospital except for the birth of my five babies. I had always been in pretty good health, and never suffered from fear. I was always the one preaching faith to the fearful and building people up when they were down! Now here I was in a situation where I lost total control. I just kept praying and quoting the Word! That's all I had to stand on, but it kept me from falling apart.

When the ambulance team came, their procedure was a first for me. There I was in my pajamas, with hair flowing down my back, being carried to an ambulance on a stretcher, and then rushing through the night with sirens blaring, speeding to Lodi Memorial Hospital. They immediately gave me medication and did a CAT scan, which diagnosed me with a ministroke from three areas of bleeding on the brain. It may have been "mini" to them, but it was major to me! My whole life changed!

While I lay in the hospital after the scan, another episode of numbness started happening. My son and grandson were by my bed, and I insisted that they pray earnestly. I prayed and spoke in tongues and then started quoting Psalms 34 and 23, and God began to touch me. Those around me could see when He did because the lip that was drooping slightly, recovered and I was able to talk normally.

I began a journey down a road I had never walked. Later that evening, the medical staff transferred me to UC Davis Hospital in Sacramento because they wanted to do an MRI (another first for me), so into a second ambulance we went. I am thankful that all my children and their spouses who lived in Stockton, California, were with me at different times at both hospitals. Elizabeth and Sherrie stayed all night with me the first night, which was very reassuring to me.

On May 8, I was supposed to be delivering a message at a church in Monterey, California, pastored by Monte Albalos. Instead I was being told that the technicians were going to do an MRI on my brain. My son and daughter had been telling me what to expect—the strange clicking noises, the long wait for it to be over while one couldn't move but had to be still—so I started praying and asking God to help me because I felt fearful. Suddenly, God spoke a verse of Scripture to me that became like a refrain:

> Fear thou not; for I am with thee: be not dismayed;
> for I am thy God: I will strengthen thee; yea, I will
> help thee; yea, I will uphold thee with the right
> hand of my righteousness. (Isaiah 41:10)

With that Word fresh in my mind, they rolled me down the long corridor toward the testing room. The young men who assisted me were kind but emphatic about not moving during the test. They put me in the coffin-like machine and it all started. It was a strange, desolate experience accompanied by clicking sounds and weird noises. I prayed silently and began to quote the passage God had given me as well as the twenty-third psalm. As I prayed and quoted the Word, tears ran down the sides of my face, wetting my hair, and I couldn't wipe them away. Strangely, I felt God's presence come inside that cubicle in which I was encased, and His Word comforted me. It was strength to me when I felt so alone.

IN THE FIRST THREE WEEKS, I WAS RUSHED BACK TO THE HOSPITAL SEVERAL TIMES;

I quoted this verse of Scripture during the MRI, after it, and many days after going home from the hospital. When fear came, I quoted it. When symptoms tried to come back, I quoted it. I literally lived and breathed the Word of God over and over for days and months, memorizing and quoting numerous verses and passages of Scripture. That power helped me through the dark trial.

In the first three weeks, I was rushed back to the hospital several times; I rode in six different ambulances, underwent CAT scans, and was a puzzle to the doctors. They couldn't believe my responses were so strong when they tested, poked, and prodded me to do different things. I had no clue where God was leading me but was assured over and over that He was with me, even though I did not like this new pathway He was leading me down.

But now I know I was not qualified in 2014 to write the book He spoke to me to write, because I hadn't gone low enough. Through all the things in my past and all the pain and distress, God helped me to be strong.

I have said for years, "You have to bleed to bless!" It's not something you choose to do, but when you do, you know that "all things work together for good to them that love God, to them who are the called according to his purpose" (Romans 8:28).

> Amid my list of blessings infinite,
> Stands this the foremost,
> "That my heart has bled."
> –EDWARD YOUNG [1]

Many people through the ages have done their best work when great adversity came.

> It was not until Beethoven had become so deaf he could not hear the fortissimo of a full orchestra that he composed his chief oratorio. It was not until John Milton had become stone blind that he could dictate the sublimest poem of the ages. It was not until Walter Scott was kicked by a horse and confined to the house for many days that he could write the "Lay of the Last Minstrel." The painter who mixes his colors with blood from his own broken heart makes the best pictures. The mightiest men [and women] of all ages have been mightiest in their agonies. —TALMAGE [2]

I know it takes more than bleeding to do some things. It's suffering so deep you feel terrorized by Hell, and you cry out to God with such urgency and desperation, knowing that He is your only hope when your strength is gone!

The following chapters will deal with the whys and help you understand how God is such an integral part of His children's lives.

We all ask why at times:

- Jeremiah: "Why am I in this filthy pit?"
- Job: "Why all the loss and pain?"
- David: "Why must I run for my life?"
- Abraham: "Why am I asked to sacrifice the promise?"
- Paul: "Why so much persecution and pain?"
- John the Baptist: "Why must I die so young, with such a gruesome death?"

Answer:
"As for God, his way is perfect" (Psalm 18:30).

1
BROUGHT LOW

For I know the thoughts that I think toward you,
saith the Lord, thoughts of peace, and not of evil,
to give you an expected end.
–Jeremiah 29:11

What does it mean to be brought low? Psalm 107:39 starts out, "Again, they are minished and brought low." Regarding the word low, Albert Barnes writes, "The Hebrew literally means to hang down, to be pendulous, to swing, to wave – as a bucket in a well, or as the slender branches of the palm, the willow, etc. Then it means to be slack, feeble, weak, as in sickness, etc." (*Barnes' Notes on the Old and New Testaments*). Scripture offers numerous other examples of being brought low:

> Thou, which hast shewed me great and sore troubles, shalt quicken me again, and shalt bring me up again from the depths of the earth. (Psalm 71:20)

> He brought me up also out of an horrible pit, out of the miry clay, and set my feet upon a rock, and established my goings. (Psalm 40:2)

> Thou hast laid me in the lowest pit, in darkness, in the deeps. (Psalm 88:6)

God is, and He alone rules. Paul affirms the sovereignty of God in I Timothy 6:15: "Which in his times he shall shew, who is the blessed and only Potentate, the King of kings, and Lord of lords."

God is sovereign, sees all things, knows all things, and there is no limit to His power. He sees every sparrow that falls to the ground. He is aware and knows about everything you do, as David proclaimed:

> Thou compassest my path and my lying down, and art acquainted with all my ways. (Psalm 139:3)

> You saw me before I was born. Every day of my life was recorded in your book. Every moment was laid out before a single day had passed. (Psalm 139:16, NLT)

God owns us! We are His property and He protects what is His! "What? know ye not that your body is the temple of the Holy Ghost . . . and ye are not your own? For ye are bought with a price: therefore glorify God in your body, and in your spirit, which are God's" (I Corinthians 6:19–20).

Nothing can touch you without God's permission! Only what God allows to happen will happen! "We can make our plans, but the LORD determines our steps" (Proverbs 16:9, NLT).

God is so emphatic about this that He thundered from the heavens and spoke to an arrogant heathen king. King Nebuchadnezzar spoke, "Is not this great Babylon, that I have built for the house of the kingdom by the might of my power, and for the honour of my majesty?" (Daniel 4:30).

NOTHING CAN TOUCH YOU WITHOUT GOD'S PERMISSION!

While he was still speaking, God spoke to the king, saying, "The kingdom is departed from thee. And they shall drive thee from men, and thy dwelling shall be with the beasts of the field: they shall make thee to eat grass as oxen, and seven times shall pass over thee, until thou know that the most High ruleth in the kingdom of men, and giveth it to whomsoever he will." God brought Nebuchadnezzar low. After his experience suffering a form of temporary insanity, God restored his health, and at the end of his days he "blessed the most High" and "praised and honoured him that liveth for ever."

Back to my story:

When I arrived home from the hospital, a brand-new life awaited me. The one everyone leaned on (me) was now in the bed and needed help with everything. Our youngest daughter dragged a twin-size mattress into my bedroom and slept on the floor by my bed where she could listen and watch my every move.

For the first two months she hardly even slept; it was a scary time for both of us. When my blood pressure escalated, she would run downstairs to the kitchen and juice organic celery for me, often at 2:00 or 3:00 in the morning. That always seemed to help. It was a stressful time, and we both had trouble sleeping.

When someone is going through difficult and trying times, it is critical to have a prayer covering. I am forever grateful for all the prayers to God on my behalf by so many precious, dedicated prayer warriors from near and far. Their prayers were worth more than gold!

The following story illustrates the importance of a prayer covering:

One missionary, who believed mission work could not succeed without prayer support, said it this way: "Unprayed for, I feel like a diver on the bottom of the river with no connecting line to the surface, and no air to breathe; or like a fireman with an empty hose on a burning building. With prayer, I feel like David facing Goliath!"[1]

During the first six months of my recovery, before my blood pressure was stabilized, God graciously gave me wonderful children whom we could call or text for prayer. I am thankful for them all. We woke all of them at various times, but we weren't always able to get hold of all of them, especially during the night. I give special thanks to Tim and

Sherrie Moran. They kept their phone right by them, and when Angela would call or text asking them to join us in prayer, they would rouse themselves and send up powerful prayers

One special young man of God, evangelist Josh Herring, became a powerful prayer warrior for me during this time. It all started on May 8, 2016, when I was released from intensive care. When they opened the big double doors to wheel me downstairs, there he stood. I was shocked and overwhelmed with thanksgiving. He held my hand as they wheeled me to my daughter's car, and then he prayed a strong prayer for me before we left the hospital to drive home. His parting words were, "Sister Haney, promise me you will call me whether day or night when you need somebody to pray for you!"

When terror began to overtake me, my blood pressure escalated dangerously high, and symptoms started coming back, my body would go in shock, and I'd tell Angela, "Text Brother Josh Herring to pray!" And pray he did, powerful fervent prayers. Always concerned, he wouldn't stop praying until things were normalized.

At my first doctor's visit, a month after the initial health crisis, the physician told me to start walking thirty minutes a day, five days a week, to help speed the healing process. We have a two-story home and upstairs is a walkway around part of the family room which is open, so I could see down into it. With three bay windows, I could see for miles all the surrounding countryside. I started walking slowly and steadily, all the while praying to Jesus. During that time, tears were ever present as I missed my beloved husband. I wished he was there to walk with me through all this. It was as if my life was put on hold for a season! I had to have groceries delivered, my children (Elizabeth and Sherrie mainly) had to drive me to doctors' appointments, and for a long while, I couldn't go to church. But when God finally gave me strength to go to church, my husband's sister, Shirley, picked me up, took me to church, and drove me back home. I am thankful for everyone who helped carry me through this low period. It was a path I would not have chosen, but the Lord, my Shepherd, led me down it! I was stripped, crushed, and brought low, and there were moments when terror would begin to overtake me. Oh how I prayed and quoted the Word of God, fighting for my strength and healing!

This was a new path for me. I couldn't write books or travel, and I had to cancel speaking engagements. Everything was put on hold because of the effects of the ministroke on my nervous system. I lost so much weight; I was a shadow of myself. My children were all worried about me.

One day as I was walking, praying, and feeling sad, I saw a flutter outside the window. A sparrow sat on the porch roof right by where I was walking. Because it appeared every day from then on, I wrote the date in my Bible, June 2016, because I knew God had sent the sparrow to speak to me. This began the lesson of the sparrow that God was bringing to me. Every day after that when I would walk, the sparrow would come. One day he turned and stared at me right in the eye for the longest time. God spoke to me, "Are not two sparrows sold for a farthing? and one of them shall not fall on the ground without your Father. But the very hairs of your head are all numbered.

Fear ye not therefore, ye are of more value than many sparrows" (Matthew 10:29–31; see also Luke 12:6–7).

That powerful phrase leaped out at me, "Ye are of more value than many sparrows!" I was emotional, weeping intensely, because I felt God's presence so strong. I repeated over and over, "Ye are of more value than many sparrows!"

Sparrows are common everywhere. When David was afflicted, he described himself as being alone like a sparrow, "I watch, and am as a sparrow alone upon the house top" (Psalm 102:7).

"YE ARE OF MORE VALUE THAN MANY SPARROWS!"

The sparrow saga continued. Every time I would go out on the deck, a sparrow would fly to where I was. For several months, the sparrow was a sign to me that God was ordering my steps. He was with me! Oh! The sweet communion with my Savior!

One day His presence was so thick and so strong I saw Him high and lifted up. I fell to my knees and cried as Isaiah cried, "Woe is me!" I saw a vision of fire coming from His throne and I prayed, "Let the fire of God come and burn up anything in my body that shouldn't be there! Make me whole by Your mighty power!"

During this time I repented of everything I could think of. I was brought low and stayed low at His feet much of the time during the healing process. He frequently brought to my mind the old song, "I See a Crimson Stream of Blood," which I sang often:

On Cal'vry's hill of sorrow
Where sin's demands were paid,
And rays of hope for tomorrow
Across our path were laid.

Refrain: I see a crimson stream of blood,
It flows from Calvary,
Its waves which reach the throne of God,
Are sweeping over me.

Today no condemnation
Abides to turn away
My soul from His salvation,
He's in my heart to stay.

Refrain

When gloom and sadness whisper,
"You've sinned—no use to pray,"
I look away to Jesus,
And He tells me to say:

Refrain

And when we reach the portal
Where life forever reigns,
The ransomed hosts' grand final
Will be this glad refrain.

For several months God sent that sparrow to visit me
as a reminder of His great love and care. I would text my

girls and tell them about this phenomenon. It became such a part of my life that I began to do a study on sparrows. If you would like to read more about them, there is a wonderful article by Rob Dunn at the Smithsonian website. [2]

In all this time, I marveled at how small humans are in comparison to the great God! Consider the following examples:

We are but grasshoppers. "It is he that sitteth upon the circle of the earth, and the inhabitants thereof are as grasshoppers" (Isaiah 40:22).

We are blades of grass. Psalm 103:15–16: "As for man, his days are as grass: as a flower of the field, so he flourisheth. For the wind passeth over it, and it is gone." First Peter 1:24: "For all flesh is as grass, and all the glory of man as the flower of grass. The grass withereth, and the flower thereof falleth away."

We are dust of the earth. "And the LORD God formed man of the dust of the ground, and breathed into his nostrils the breath of life; and man became a living soul" (Genesis 2:7).

Despite our low stature in comparison with Him, God chose us to be His friends. We weren't lowly grass and grasshoppers in His sight. Jesus brought those who would accept His commands into a new, close relationship with Him: "Ye are my friends, if ye do whatsoever I command you. Henceforth I call you not servants; for the servant knoweth not what his lord doeth: but I have called you friends; for all things that I have heard of my Father I have made known unto you" (John 15:14–15). The Lord has also made us His sons and daughters. "And I will be your Father, and you will be my sons and daughters, says the LORD Almighty" (II Corinthians 6:18, NLT; see also I John 3:1–2).

Ephesians 2:6 shows our position of elevation as we sit with Christ: "And hath raised us up together, and made us sit together in heavenly places in Christ Jesus." You can be in a sick bed and be in a heavenly place, for where His sweet presence is, it's heavenly. You can be surrounded by the darkest storm and feel like life is closing in on you, yet when you humble your heart and cry out to God, His presence comes and soothes your breaking heart. Prayer is not a position of body but a position of the heart. God hears the cry of a humble, afflicted soul whether it be in a heartfelt song or words formed in prayer.

H. G. Bosch told the following story about a song I sang during this time. He wrote, "When I was a very young boy, a dear neighbor who lived two doors down the street experienced a great sorrow. She often sang and played at her piano, but after this tragedy struck in her life, the first song with which she would open her 'daily concert' was the lovely hymn, 'I Must Tell Jesus.' The words made a deep impression upon me as a child."[3]

Psalm 18 describes what happens when we cry to God: "He bowed the heavens also, and came down: and darkness was under his feet. . . . He took me, he drew me out of many waters. He delivered me from my strong enemy. . . . He brought me forth also into a large place; he delivered me, because he delighted in me" (Psalm 18:9, 16–17, 19).

During the days of my time of healing, Psalm 18 was one of the psalms I quoted often. I loved to say, "He rides on the wings of the wind!" (See verse 10.) Winter winds will rock our world. Boisterous, angry winds will blow across our normal activities and interrupt our schedule. What we do with the winds determines our destiny. No matter what happens, it is important to trust Jesus to help you and keep you from sinking into the doldrums of despair, depression, and discouragement.

Winds will come, but they are intended to strengthen:

No tree becomes rooted and sturdy unless many a wind assails it. For by its very tossing it tightens its grip and plants its roots more securely; the fragile trees are those that have grown in a sunny valley. –SENECA THE YOUNGER[4]

There is an interesting story about wind in Matthew 14:22–33. Jesus told His disciples to get into a ship and go to the other side while He sent the multitudes away. He told them He would join them later. Having sent the multitude away, Jesus went into the mountains to pray alone. In the meantime, the ship in which the disciples were traveling entered a storm. The disciples were frightened when they saw Jesus walking on the water.

NO MATTER WHAT HAPPENS . . . TRUST JESUS TO HELP YOU

But Jesus said, "Be of good cheer; it is I; be not afraid."

This is when Peter said, "Lord, if it's You, bid me come into the water with You!"

Jesus said, "Come!"

Peter got out of the boat and started walking on the water! But when he saw the boisterous wind, he was afraid. When he began to sink, he cried out, "Lord, save me!"

Jesus grabbed his outstretched hand and saved him from the angry waves. Together they walked toward the ship. When Jesus got in the ship with them, the wind ceased.

Jesus knew about the storm. He allowed the storm to come and the wind to blow, but He was with them during their fear and during the blowing of the wind. The wind didn't cease when He came near to them. It only stopped when He got into the ship. This displays God's timing.

So many lessons lay in this one small story:

1. When Jesus sent them ahead of Him, He knew there would be a wind before there was a wind. He knows every detail of our lives before it happens.

2. Jesus was teaching them not to be afraid, even when contrary winds blow. He will take care of us no matter how bad things get! Jesus will not let us sink or go under.

3. Peter had great faith. At least he left the boat and started walking on the water. He was willing to risk all because He believed.

4. Peter didn't look at the waves; he looked at the wind. The wind is what got him off track, and he would have sunk if it hadn't been for Jesus' mercy and kindness. At one moment Peter thought he was going under, but Jesus had His eye on Peter every moment. He was not going to let him sink.

5. When Jesus told them to go across the sea to the other side, He was not speaking idle words. Jesus

made sure they would get to the other side. He didn't warn them ahead of time there would be a severe storm because He wanted to teach them a lesson in faith.

I always say: "I don't believe what I see; I believe what He said!" When troubles surround you and contrary winds blow, remember He flies on "the wings of the wind" (Psalm 18:10). He's right there with you in the storm.

When the storm blew into my life in the form of a health crisis, I couldn't control the wind, but God could. My life was in His hands. I did my best to speak faith even when I didn't feel like it. I was trying to follow the faith of Abraham from Romans 4:17 and 20, believing God to call "those things which be not as though they were" and "staggering not at the promise of God through unbelief."

The Lord God has full control of the storms and can rebuke the sea at His command. He is a stronghold when there is nothing left to hang on to, and He becomes that place of refuge to run into and hide until the storm passes over. (See Nahum 1:3-4, 7.)

God is the master of the wind; He created it. Imagine God in a chariot, flying on the wings of the wind. When the wind blows into your life, look for God in the wind. He is there watching over you and taking care of you. He knows what is best for us. As Charles Spurgeon wrote, "We need winds and tempests to exercise our faith, to tear off the rotten bough of self-dependence, and to root us more firmly in Christ."[5]

During any storm of life, the Holy Ghost is the Comforter. "Come to me, all of you who are weary and carry heavy burdens, and I will give you rest"

(Matthew 11:28, NLT). "And I will pray the Father, and he shall give you another Comforter, that he may abide with you for ever. . . . But the Comforter, which is the Holy Ghost, whom the Father will send in my name, he shall teach you all things, and bring all things to your remembrance, whatsoever I have said unto you. Peace I leave with you, my peace I give unto you: not as the world giveth, give I unto you. Let not your heart be troubled, neither let it be afraid" (John 14:16, 26–27).

Recently I've been going through stacks of papers, old manuscripts, and tons of old records. One of the items I found was an email dated February 23, 1999, from my friend, the late Gwyn Oakes. I felt impressed to share her story in this book to show how God cares about His children even to the tiniest details. She entitled it, "Because He Is God."

> We had just returned home after being away for a week, and while we were unpacking, the phone rang. It was the police department in Houston, Texas. They told us they had found our son's car abandoned on the side of the road and could not locate him anywhere. They had been trying to locate us for three days to let us know they had the car and to notify us that he was missing. Our phone number was the only contact number in the car, and they were concerned that harm had befallen him.
>
> We immediately got back in the car and started for Houston. Our son had been working in the Houston area, and we had not heard from him

in about two weeks, which was not unusual. We tried calling his apartment, but no one answered. As we drove the ten hours from our home in central Arkansas, we prayed that we would find him and he would be all right.

It was after midnight when we arrived at the outskirts of Houston. We stopped to get gas and ask for directions to the police station that had called us. While my husband was getting gas, I looked over the city which seemed so vast and overwhelming. It seemed there were a million lights, each representing people. How, I wondered, would we ever find our son in this huge area? I felt so small and insignificant; then suddenly I felt the presence of the Lord. I said, "Because You are God, You know all things and You know where our son is. We don't want to leave until we locate him. Please give us directions, Lord!"

When my husband returned, I felt calm and reassured. We found we were about thirty minutes from the station. He asked, "What shall we do now? We really can't do much until morning." We had already started driving in the direction we needed to go, and I felt like we needed to turn into a convenience store. I said, "Stop here!" He asked why, and I did not know why. I just felt compelled to stop.

When we stopped in front of the store, we saw our nephew, Jim, inside. We had no idea he lived in Houston. My husband walked inside, and Jim looked at him so strangely and said, "What are you doing down here?" My husband said, "I will ask you, what are you doing here?" He replied, "I have wanted a Coke since 9:00 tonight and finally couldn't stand it any longer. I got out of bed and came over here to get a Coke. The strange thing is, I don't even like Coke."

We told him why we were there, and he said, "Oh, I know where David is. His job moved, and his car quit on the side of the road. So he asked me to come and pick it up for him since I was so near, and he continued the trip with a friend. I went to get the car, but when I got there, the car was gone. I've been really concerned how to tell him the car was gone."

I told him how I had prayed that we would find David, and that we didn't know where to start. After I explained that the Lord had given him a thirst for a Coke and compelled him to get out of bed to go to the store at just the right time, he was very shaky for a while when he realized that was exactly what happened. We rejoiced in a God who knows all things.

The chance of finding someone in the middle of the night in a city the size of Houston with no other contact was impossible if God didn't orchestrate it. Because He is God, He can do all things. . . . "That thou mayest know that there is none like unto the Lord our God" (Exodus 8:10).

During the time of regaining my health, my eyes were opened to all the people in the Bible who were brought low and how God was involved in the process. Below is a partial list:

- Joseph was put in a pit without water.
- Jeremiah was lowered into a dungeon.
- Hannah was childless and in a pit of despair.
- Job experienced enormous loss and affliction.
- Jonah was cast overboard and ended up in the belly of a large fish.
- Paul was imprisoned.
- David was thrown in a pit (II Samuel 17:9) and experienced the pit of hopelessness and grief.
- Elijah was chased by a diabolical woman and said, "O LORD, take away my life" (I Kings 19:4).

When you are brought low, it could be for any of several reasons:

1. Like He did with Job, God trusts you enough to show Satan how faithful you are.
2. Like Jonah, you are running from what God told you to do.
3. God has put you on the potter's wheel.
4. As fulfillment of Scripture, "Ye shall have tribulation."
5. You were born for a purpose that many people couldn't do or wouldn't want to do.
6. This is for His kingdom's sake.
7. To prepare you for a purpose that only God in His foreknowledge can see happening at a later date.

8. So you will see Him in a greater measure than before.

You may not understand all that is happening during an intense trial, but God moves with purpose. I don't understand everything, but I will always remember how I saw God high and lifted up like never before, and how He came to me during some of my lowest days; how He vividly taught me the lesson of the sparrow, and how much more He cares about every detail of our lives. <u>The main ingredient during a trial is to trust in God no matter what</u>!

Never be afraid to trust an unknown future to a known God.
–CORRIE TEN BOOM

2

RESTORED FOR
HIS NAME'S SAKE

Be still, my soul: the Lord is on thy side. Bear patiently the cross of grief or pain. Leave to thy God to order and provide; In every change, He faithful will remain.
–Katarina A. von Schlegel[1]

His name is highly exalted above all the billions of people on the earth. A name of power and deliverance, it is highly feared by Hell and its inhabitants. His name is the highest authority in the earth, the heavens, and the whole universe.

"Wherefore God also hath highly exalted him, and given him a name which is above every name: that at the name of Jesus every knee should bow, of things in heaven, and things in earth, and things under the earth." (Philippians 2:9–10)

Worldwide inhabitants of the earth, every being in Heaven, and every person in the universe will bow in honor to the hallowed name of Jesus. He said He would lead us in the right paths so His name would be exalted and glorified in everything we do.

Even in the Lord's Prayer the name is referred to as hallowed, which means to be revered as sacred and holy. The Kingdom is His. He has all power. If anyone has any power, He gave it to that person and allowed him or her to have it.

The prophet Isaiah wrote about the magnitude of His name and what it embodied: "His name shall be called Wonderful, Counsellor, The mighty God, The everlasting Father, The Prince of Peace" (Isaiah 9:6).

The heavenly hosts fear and revere that name. The Lord Himself honors those who talk about and think about His name. He has a special place reserved for those who do. "Then they that feared the LORD spake often one to another: and the LORD hearkened, and heard it, and a book of remembrance was written before him for them that feared the LORD, and that thought upon his name" (Malachi 3:16).

King David understood the majesty of God's name and wrote much about worship unto Him. The story of David begins when Samuel the prophet anointed David to be king. It was a special moment in David's life: "And he sent, and brought him in. Now he was ruddy, and withal of a beautiful countenance, and goodly to look to. And the Lord said, Arise, anoint him: for this is he. Then Samuel took the horn of oil, and anointed him in the midst of his brethren: and the Spirit of the Lord came upon David from that day forward" (I Samuel 16:12–13).

David was the youngest son of Jesse, a Judean from Bethlehem who was the son of Obed and the grandson of Boaz. During a war with the Philistines, David was sent by his father with a present for his three brothers, who were serving in Saul's army in the valley of Elah. As he approached the camp, he heard the thundering, defiant words of the giant, Goliath of Gath, "I defy the armies of Israel this day; give me a man, that we may fight together" (I Samuel 17:10). When David started asking questions about the man, his brothers reproached him and told him to go home. Instead, David started asking the other soldiers about the reward King Saul promised the one who could kill the giant.

Something stirred within David, and he started talking, saying that he would fight the giant. David had confidence in his own abilities (he told Saul that he had killed a bear and a lion with his bare hands), but he was more confident in God. He told Saul, "The LORD that delivered me out of the paw of the lion, and out of the paw of the bear, he will deliver me out of the hand of this Philistine" (I Samuel 17:37).

At the time of the battle, David announced his trust in the name of the Lord when he said to Goliath, "Thou comest to me with a sword, and with a spear, and with a shield: but I come to thee in the name of the LORD of hosts, the God of the armies of Israel, whom thou hast defied" (I Samuel 17:45). It was David's confident trust in God and His name that gave him the victory.

Why did the Lord say David was a man after his own heart? (See Acts 13:22.) David committed adultery, premeditated murder, and he disobeyed God's command not to number the people! So why did he have a special place with God?

1. David as a young man had faith in God and recognized His power and majesty, which is reflected in his psalms.

2. God was with David, and Saul recognized it. "And Saul was afraid of David, because the LORD was with him, and was departed from Saul" (I Samuel 18:12; see also I Samuel 18:14–15, 28–29).

3. David had a humble, repentant spirit when dealt with by the prophets. At the end of the pronouncement that the son born to him by Bathsheba was going to die, David lay on the ground seven days and nights, fasting and asking God for mercy. But on the seventh day the child died. "Then David arose from the earth, and washed, and anointed himself, and changed his apparel, and came into the house of the LORD, and worshipped" (II Samuel 12:20).

The third sin he committed was disobedience to God. "And David's heart smote him after that he had numbered the people. And David said unto the LORD, I have sinned greatly in that I have done: and now, I beseech thee, O LORD, take away the iniquity of thy servant; for I have done very foolishly" (II Samuel 24:10). Again he was repentant and also an honorable man as shown by how he took the punishment. "David spake unto the LORD when he saw the angel that smote the people, and said, Lo, I have sinned, and I have done wickedly: but these sheep, what have they done? let thine hand, I pray thee, be against me, and against my father's house" (II Samuel 24:17). God told him to build an altar in the threshingfloor of Araunah, which he did, and then the Lord relented (II Samuel 24:24–25).

King David knew much pain and suffering in his life from the anger and rejection shown to him by King Saul to the pain of his own sins and the judgments associated with them. For approximately twenty years David was chased like a mad dog and had to run for his life from a deranged king. David had been anointed to be king, but it was many years before that happened. Because of him, generation after generation has been blessed by the verses in Psalms that God inspired him to write.

The Book of Psalms "brings us into the sanctuary, draws us off from converse with men, and directs us into communion with God, by solacing and reposing our souls in him, lifting up and letting out our hearts towards him. . . . The penman of most of them was David the son of Jesse, who is therefore called the sweet palmist of Israel, II Samuel 23:1."[2]

In the thirty-eighth psalm David cried: "I am troubled; I am bowed down greatly; I go mourning all the day long. . . . I am feeble and sore broken: I have roared by reason of the disquietness of my heart. . . . My heart panteth, my strength faileth me: as for the light of mine eyes, it also is gone from me. . . . But I, as a deaf man, heard not; and I was as a dumb man that openeth not his mouth" (Psalm 38:6, 8, 10, 13). It was a psalm of repentance and grief. Not only was he sick and afflicted, but even his friends had deserted him. He was persecuted by his enemies.

In Psalm 22:1–2, he cried: "My God, my God, why hast thou forsaken me? why art thou so far from helping me, and from the words of my roaring? O my God, I cry in the daytime, but thou hearest not; and in the night season, and am not silent."

But the thread that ran through his life was his deep hunger for God and his reverence and honor toward Him. David did have a heart after God. It showed in his writings and songs. When he was in the wilderness of Judah, he cried, "O God, thou art my God; early will I seek thee: my soul thirsteth for thee, my flesh longeth for thee in a dry and thirsty land, where no water is" (Psalm 63:1).

"O GOD, THOU ART MY GOD; EARLY WILL I SEEK THEE." (PSALM 63:1)

He trusted his God to help him and cried in Psalm 116:6: "The LORD preserveth the simple: I was brought low, and he helped me."

Gill's Exposition of the Entire Bible comments on this verse,

> The psalmist returns to his own case, and gives an instance of the divine goodness in himself; he had been brought low by affliction of body, by distress of enemies, through want of the necessaries and conveniences of life; he had been brought low as to spiritual things, through the weakness of grace, the prevalence of corruption, the temptations of Satan, and the hidings of God's face; but the Lord helped him to bear up under all this; he

put underneath his everlasting arms, and upheld him with the right hand of his righteousness; he helped him out of his low estate, and delivered him out of all his troubles, when none else could; when things were at the greatest extremity, and he in the utmost distress, just ready to go down into silence and dwell there.

Psalm 28:1 says, "Unto thee will I cry, O LORD, my rock; be not silent to me: lest, if thou be silent to me, I become like them that go down into the pit."

When you have despairing, hopeless thoughts, dark-ness surrounds you, the bottom has dropped out of your world, seemingly your dreams have died, and tears form a river of sadness—the only one who can help you in the depths of your soul is the One who said, "Let there be light," and there was light. Jesus wants to speak light into your darkness, bring joy where there is sadness, give hope where there is desolation, heal, and restore you. I have literally quoted the twenty-third psalm every day since May 6, 2016.

Once a pastor phoned the local editor of religious news and gave him the topic for his Sunday message, "The Lord is my Shepherd." The editor asked, "Is that all?" The pastor replied, "That's enough." The editor, thinking that was part of his subject, announced the pastor's topic as "The Lord is my Shepherd; that's enough." To know the Lord as our protector and provider is enough to allay all fears and soothe all our sorrows.[3]

Psalm 23. A Psalm of David.

The LORD is my shepherd; I shall not want. He maketh me to lie down in green pastures: he leadeth me beside the still waters. He restoreth my soul: he leadeth me in the paths of righteousness for his name's sake. Yea, though I walk through the valley of the shadow of death, I will fear no evil: for thou art with me; thy rod and thy staff they comfort me. Thou preparest a table before me in the presence of mine enemies: thou anointest my head with oil; my cup runneth over. Surely goodness and mercy shall follow me all the days of my life: and I will dwell in the house of the LORD for ever.

IN THE VALLEY

Everyone sooner or later will go through a valley experience. For many people, it will not be just one time but many times. When life is good and all is well, there is not the urgent need to spend as much time in prayer with Jesus, but when trouble comes, where is the first place we go? When pain, heartache, or problems force us to our knees, that is the best position in which to pray and pour out our heart to Jesus, the only one who truly cares and understands completely. He is our Father, and we can approach Him as His children, telling Him all about it, sobbing until we cannot cry any more, and praying until we have victory. Then we get the Bible out and pray the Word, something that pertains to our situation. We need to look at things through the eyes of God and His Word. He will not fail you! Neither will He let you suffer alone! He is walking with you, and sometimes when the trial becomes too heavy for you to bear, He will carry you.

Yes, every Christian will walk through some low places, some impossible to get out of, but God makes the difference. He will help you.

"Thou hast delivered my soul from death, mine eyes from tears, and my feet from falling. I will walk before the LORD in the land of the living" (Psalm 116:8-9).

Then say with Job, "Though God slay me, yet will I trust Him!" Quote Micah 7:7-8: "Therefore I will look unto the LORD: I will wait for the God of my salvation: my God will hear me. Rejoice not against me, O mine enemy; when I fall, I shall arise; when I sit in darkness, the LORD shall be a light unto me."

Micah the prophet said, "I will wait for God." This is a difficult thing to do. It's mirrored in the story about the famous New England preacher Phillips Brooks, who was known for his "poise and imperturbability. His intimate friends, however, knew that, at times, he suffered moments of frustration and irritability. One day a friend saw him pacing the floor like a caged lion. 'What is the trouble, Dr. Brooks?' asked the friend. 'The trouble is that I'm in a hurry, but God isn't!' he answered."[4]

David expressed the agony of waiting in Psalm 6:2-6:

Have mercy upon me, O LORD; for I am weak: O LORD, heal me; for my bones are vexed. My soul is also sore vexed: but thou, O LORD, how long? Return, O LORD, deliver my soul: oh save me for thy mercies' sake. For in death there is no remembrance of thee: in the grave who shall give thee thanks? I am weary with my groaning; all the night make I my bed to swim; I water my couch with my tears.

God is with you. He will help you. God's mercies are new every morning. His Word will not fail. Tomorrow is a new day of hope. Refuse to give up. God does things that seem impossible.

When you are hardest hit is the time to keep going. Never lose hope. Samuel Smiles once said, "Hope is like the sun; as we journey toward it, it casts the shadow of our burden behind us." No matter what you're going through, hang on to the God of hope. Trials and tough times will end.

Your *I will* must be stronger than feelings. David spoke of the Lord and what He would do. Then he said even though he was in a shadowy place of death, "I will fear no evil." "I will dwell in the house of the LORD for ever." He said "I will" because of God's love, provisions, and promises.

God takes care of His own. His ways are above our ways. We're prone to say, "If only God would have answered sooner, this wouldn't have happened!" The same words were spoken by Mary in John 11:32, "Lord, if thou hadst been here, my brother had not died." God knows what's best, and He sees the bigger picture from a higher point of view.

When we reach the end of our rope and feel like we can't hold on another moment, God is there waiting with open arms to catch us. When it seems like there is no way,

He makes a way. He's never late but always on time, even when we think He's not.

God has not abandoned you. It is normal to feel abandoned when your trial goes on for a long time. You are not alone in feeling this way, as shown in Isaiah 49:14: "But Zion said, The LORD hath forsaken me, and my Lord hath forgotten me."

God responded, "Can a woman forget her sucking child, that she should not have compassion on the son of her womb? yea, they may forget, yet will I not forget thee. Behold, I have graven thee upon the palms

GOD HAS NOT ABANDONED YOU.

of my hands; thy walls are continually before me" (Isaiah 49:15–16).

We are vessels He can flow through. Our trials make us strong. Pearls are made by abrasive sand. A butterfly emerges after intense struggle; diamonds require cutting and polishing. Have faith in God during the storms of life. Losses will come, but He is with you.

"Fret not! Trust in the Lord" (Psalm 37).

"Fear not! I am with you!" (Isaiah 41:10).

"Faint not! Always pray" (Luke 18:1).

In Psalm 23 the paths of righteousness are the ways of obedience, becoming more like Him. Why does He lead me in the paths of righteousness? So that He will get the glory for the sake of His name.

He works with us, molding, shaping, loving, and caring for us. Revelation 19:11 tells us His name is "Faithful and True." He is faithful in His ministrations toward us.

In the New Testament we are His namesake. When we are born again in Christ Jesus, we take on His name. He will fight fiercely to keep us as His own and will do whatever He needs to do so we can bring glory to His name.

Valleys and the shadow of death sometimes bring this about! When we lose control, He is in control if we allow Him to be. It's a time of learning, repenting, and humbling ourselves before Him.

We were purchased with His blood. We bear His name. We are His namesake. We must become like the One whose name we bear. "What? know ye not that your body is the temple of the Holy Ghost which is in you, which ye have of God, and ye are not your own? For ye are bought with a price: therefore glorify God in your body, and in your spirit, which are God's" (I Corinthians 6:19–20).

A namesake is a person named for another person—for the sake of the other's name, to keep it alive.

In Job's case, the name of God and His kingdom were glorified, and Satan was shown the glory and power of God through Job's humility and allegiance to Almighty God in spite of his being brought low, sitting on an ash pile and scraping his boil-covered body.

One person's trial can be an unexpected blessing to many, as demonstrated in the following story:

> Years ago, a fishing fleet went out from a small harbor on the east coast of Newfoundland. In the afternoon there came up a great storm. When night settled down, not a single vessel of all the fleet had found its way into port. All night long wives, mothers, children, and sweethearts paced

up and down the beach, wringing their hands and calling on God to save their loved ones. To add to the horror of the situation, one of the cottages caught fire. Since the men were all away, it was impossible to save the home. When the morning broke, to the joy of all, the entire fleet found safe harbor in the bay. But there was one face that was a picture of despair, the wife of the man whose home had been destroyed. Meeting her husband as he landed, she cried, "Oh! husband, we are ruined. Our house and all it contained was destroyed by the fire!" But the man exclaimed, "Thank God for the fire! It was the light of the burning cottage that guided the whole fleet into port!"[5]

Always remember in every trial, Romans 8:28 is true: "And we know that all things work together for good."

First Peter 5:10: "But the God of all grace, who hath called us unto his eternal glory by Christ Jesus, after that ye have suffered a while, make you perfect, stablish, strengthen, settle you."

I like the phrase in Zechariah, "prisoners of hope." Zechariah 9:12: "Turn you to the strong hold, ye prisoners of hope: even to day do I declare that I will render double unto thee."

Jesus came to bring abundant life and deliverance; He has great plans for His children as stated in Jeremiah 29:11: "For I know the thoughts that I think toward you, saith the LORD, thoughts of peace, and not of evil, to give you an expected end."

"And I will restore to you the years that the locust hath eaten, the cankerworm, and the caterpiller, and the palmer-worm, my great army which I sent among you. And ye shall eat in plenty, and be satisfied, and praise the name of the LORD your God, that hath dealt wondrously with you: and my people shall never be ashamed" (Joel 2:25–26).

Jeremiah 30:17: "For I will restore health unto thee, and I will heal thee of thy wounds, saith the LORD; because they called thee an Outcast, saying, This is Zion, whom no man seeketh after."

It's encouraging to see the three faces of faith that were displayed when three women were brought low:

1. The Shunammite woman went into the pit of death, and cried, "Give me back my son who is dead!" (See II Kings 4.)
2. The lady with the issue of blood suffered the lowly dregs of an incurable disease and pushed her way through the crowd so she could touch the hem of Jesus' garment by faith! "If I can just touch His garment, I shall be made whole!" (See Matthew 9.)
3. The Syrophenician lady went into a pit of demonic activity suffered by her daughter. "Truth, Lord, yet the dogs eat of the crumbs." (See Matthew 15.)

All three women had something in common. They would not let go until God gave them their miracle.

Though Hell come against you, boisterous winds threaten, the night is long, and treacherous waves of despair try to drown you, know that somewhere in the shadowy darkness, Jesus will come walking on the stormy sea of your life. He will speak: "Peace, be still. It is I; be not afraid!" He will restore you for His name's sake.

Know that your trial will not be wasted, for it is promised in II Corinthians 1:3–4: "Blessed be God, even the Father of our Lord Jesus Christ, the Father of mercies, and the God of all comfort; who comforteth us in all our tribulation, that we may be able to comfort them which are in any trouble, by the comfort wherewith we ourselves are comforted of God."

When I was just a young girl, I dedicated my life to God and would pray, "Use me, Jesus, for Your glory!" I never realized He was going to use me in my weakened condition to bring people to the realization of their place in God and growth in their spiritual walk. During my time of healing, several ministers told me that the trial I went through strengthened them and increased their boldness in prayer, enabling them to take authority in spiritual warfare. Two of their testimonies are as follows:

Evangelist Josh Herring wrote:

Sister Haney, it's an honor to speak these words to you out of my heart. Who would have thought that the Lord would have chosen this chapter of your life to be the chapter of war? War should have been in the beginning or in the middle stages of your ministry but not this stage in life. This should have been the stage where spoils of war were being received, but God has chosen you to be able to go through one more battle. What a victory you have accomplished, and to do it alone is unbelievable! But for the hand of our God who has been with you is astounding. He chose you to be an eagle and to soar above the storms, which most people would just view from the ground, afraid to soar or flap their wings, because your wings are so much stronger than everyone else around you.

One day I desire to have wings like yours, to be able to fly in the heights of the Spirit world like you do, and to hear the voice of my Savior as intimately as you do. Thank you for displaying to my generation such strength, fortitude, power, and perseverance in the spiritual and supernatural; we look up to you as you soar above us. You war to soar! Thank you for everything you've been as an example to my generation. Thank you for showing us we can do it! We can make it! You have bound the strong man, and the spoils of war are coming! The Lord has truly had His hand on you, and I will say this: with this war you have been through and this victory you've had to fight all alone, the spoils from this war are greater than any spoils you have received before!

Tim Moran, my son-in-law, pastor of Life Church, under the auspices of Pastor John Shivers:

I have been thinking this week about what God has done in my life as a result of your trial and affliction. Your desperate situation caused me to pray with a boldness and an authority in the Holy Ghost I had not experienced before. It taught me that I had to pray with a resolute determination in the power of the name of Jesus and the authority of His Word. I learned that we had to pray until God moved. And when He moved, your need was met and the Lord's peace was present!

It reminds me when Dad preached about prevailing prayer. The church has to rise again, and pray with the boldness and confidence of David as he went against Goliath. The Lord is calling the church to pray this kind of prayer.

Also, on the Sunday after the ministroke, my son, Pastor Nathaniel Haney, told the church what happened in the hospital and how God had stopped another one before it could become full-blown. He told them he saw with his own eyes that my lip became normal again and I quoted Scripture and spoke in tongues. That day I started receiving texts, "Sister Haney, you are a miracle!" God was receiving glory for what He did!

The Christian Life Center family saw how frail and weak I was when I was finally able to come back to church. They saw a miracle unfold as they watched the progress in my health and strength while God worked in my body. He has done a miracle in me, and I will always be grateful to Him and give Him all the glory, which He so richly deserves!

I received another comforting word from dear friends in the Chicago Metro on May 11, 2016, just five days after my initial life-changing episode. The text is below:

Sister Haney:

Just a quick communique to let you know that we continue to pray for you on a very focused level. When I got news about you last Sunday, intercession hit me hard, and a vision of the angel of the Lord followed.

His sword was drawn as he stood by you. The Lord impressed me that you were safe.

Love you deeply. You are a precious mother in Zion and prayer warrior.

Ric Gonzalez
Chicago Metro

To have God and His angels with you during a health crisis is worth more than gold! It is imperative that He receives all the glory.

We shall never find happiness by looking at our prayers, our doings, or our feelings; it is what *Jesus* is, not what we are, that gives rest to the soul. —SPURGEON[6]

3
TO INCREASE HIS KINGDOM

For I reckon that the sufferings of this present time are not worthy to be compared with the glory which shall be revealed in us.
Romans 8:18

HANNAH

God let Hannah, a God-fearing woman, be brought so low that she could not eat (I Samuel 1:4–14). Finding herself in a pit of despair, she left the table where others were rejoicing and ran to the house of the Lord, crying so much that the priest assumed she was drunk. She was beside herself with grief and was at her wit's end with Elkanah's other wife who taunted her, boasting of how many kids she had. Like David in Psalm 42:3, her tears became her meat.

The Lord had shut up Hannah's womb. This caused her anguish and deep sorrow. She did not, however, get bitter at God; instead she went to the temple of the Lord to pray and cried out in bitterness of soul.

God needed a man who would become a priest and prophet, and He saw Hannah as a godly, righteous woman who would be the child's mother. He allowed her to be barren for a reason.

Hannah may have been barren and childless, but she was not prayerless. She believed in her God even in an impossible situation and needed a supernatural miracle for God to open her womb. Hannah threw herself on the mercies of the only One who could help her. "And the LORD remembered her" (I Samuel 1:19).

Hannah's prayer includes a reference to being brought low: "The LORD maketh poor, and maketh rich: he bringeth low, and lifteth up" (I Samuel 2:7). Could it be, if Hannah had many children, she would not have felt the compulsion to dedicate her son to the Lord's service? The day she was so forlorn and desperate was when she prayed that prayer of surrender.

God knew what was going to transpire in Eli's life and was preparing the next priest to fill his shoes. A man of God had told Eli that because he had allowed his sons to desecrate the temple of God, He would raise up another priest to take his place, saying, "And I will raise me up a faithful priest, that shall do according to that which is in mine heart and in my mind: and I will build him a sure house; and he shall walk before mine anointed for ever" (I Samuel 2:35). That priest was to be Samuel.

As soon as Samuel was weaned, which according to Jewish custom might not be until he was about three years old, Hannah took him to Eli, the priest of the Lord, at Shiloh. "And she said, Oh my lord, as thy soul liveth, my lord, I am the woman that stood by thee here, praying unto the LORD. For this child I prayed; and the LORD hath given me my petition which I asked of him: therefore also I have lent him to the LORD; as long as he liveth" (I Samuel 1:26–28).

Then Hannah went into the house of the Lord and prayed the following powerful prophetic prayer recorded in I Samuel 2:1–7:

> And Hannah prayed, and said, My heart rejoiceth in the LORD, mine horn is exalted in the LORD: my mouth is enlarged over mine enemies; because I rejoice in thy salvation. There is none holy as the LORD: for there is none beside thee: neither is there any rock like our God. Talk no more so exceeding proudly; let not arrogancy come out of your mouth: for the LORD is a God of knowledge, and by him actions are weighed. The bows of the mighty men are broken, and they that stumbled are girded with strength. They that were full have hired out themselves for bread; and they that were hungry ceased: so that the barren hath born seven; and she that hath many children is waxed feeble. The LORD killeth, and maketh alive: he bringeth down to the grave, and bringeth up. The LORD maketh poor, and maketh rich: he bringeth low, and lifteth up.

Yes, God brought Hannah low, but He also gave her a godly son who became a priest and prophet and also opened her womb to bear more children.

DANIEL

The account of Daniel being thrown down into the den of lions makes a good story, but who would want to experience it? The den was cold, stinky, littered with bones, and known as a place of doom and death. But God allowed Daniel to be cast to the bottom of it! While Daniel was in the pit, King Darius couldn't sleep all night because he liked and respected Daniel, and at daybreak he made his way to the den of lions and "cried with a lamentable voice . . . O Daniel, servant of the living God, is thy God, whom thou servest continually, able to deliver thee from the lions?"

Daniel replied, "O king, live for ever. My God hath sent his angel, and hath shut the lions' mouths" (Daniel 6:20–22).

"Then was the king exceeding glad for him, and commanded that they should take Daniel up out of the den. So Daniel was taken up out of the den, and no manner of hurt was found upon him, because he believed in his God" (Daniel 6:23). He was brought low, but God brought him back up!

Listen to what the king did and said:

Then king Darius wrote unto all people, nations, and languages, that dwell in all the earth. . . . I make a decree, That in every dominion of my kingdom men tremble and fear before the God of Daniel: for he is the living God, and stedfast for ever, and his kingdom that which shall not be destroyed, and his dominion shall be even unto the end. He delivereth and rescueth, and he worketh signs and wonders in heaven and in earth, who hath delivered Daniel from the power of the lions. (Daniel 6:25–27)

When Daniel was given his death sentence, he didn't panic; instead he prayed. This was against the king's decree, but the prayer that got him in trouble also brought him a miracle. Daniel's faith in God was bigger than the evil that tried to destroy him. The Lord needed a nation to turn to Him, so He allowed Daniel to be put in the lion's den.

> **WHEN DANIEL WAS GIVEN HIS DEATH SENTENCE, HE DIDN'T PANIC; INSTEAD HE PRAYED.**

THREE HEBREW CHILDREN

At another time, under the reign of a different king, God showed Himself so powerful that it shook a kingdom!

And he commanded the most mighty men that were in his army to bind Shadrach, Meshach, and Abednego, and to cast them into the burning fiery furnace. Then these men were bound in their coats, their hosen, and their hats, and their other garments, and were cast into the midst of the burning fiery furnace. Therefore because the king's commandment was urgent, and the furnace exceeding hot, the flame of the fire slew those men that took up Shadrach, Meshach, and Abednego. And these three men, Shadrach, Meshach, and Abednego, fell down bound into the midst of the burning fiery furnace.

Then Nebuchadnezzar the king was astonied, and rose up in haste, and spake, and said unto his counsellers, Did not we cast three men bound into the midst of the fire? They answered and said unto the king, True, O king. He answered and said, Lo, I see four men loose, walking in the midst of the fire, and they have no hurt; and the form of the fourth is like the Son of God. Then Nebuchadnezzar came near to the mouth of the burning fiery furnace, and spake, and said, Shadrach, Meshach, and Abednego, ye servants of the most high God, come forth, and come hither. Then Shadrach, Meshach, and Abednego, came forth of the midst of the fire. And the princes, governors, and captains, and the king's counsellers, being gathered together, saw these men, upon whose bodies the fire had no power, nor was an hair of their head singed, neither were their coats changed, nor the smell of fire had passed on them. (Daniel 3:20–27)

The devil can turn up the heat, but he can't cancel the promises! God's got His hand on the thermostat. He will not let you be destroyed. What was meant for evil, God meant for good! God received great glory for this supernatural miracle, and His kingdom was increased that day.

Then Nebuchadnezzar spake, and said, Blessed be the God of Shadrach, Meshach, and Abednego, who hath sent his angel, and delivered his servants that trusted in him, and have changed the king's word, and yielded their bodies, that they might not serve nor worship any god, except their own God. Therefore I make a decree, That every people, nation, and language, which speak any thing amiss against the God of Shadrach, Meshach, and Abednego, shall be cut in pieces, and their houses shall be made a dunghill: because there is no other God that can deliver after this sort. (Daniel 3:28–29)

Deuteronomy 4:20 is true; He can and did bring them out of the furnace: "But the LORD hath taken you, and brought you forth out of the iron furnace, even out of Egypt, to be unto him a people of inheritance, as ye are this day."

Adversity has the effect of eliciting talents, which in prosperous circumstances would have lain dormant. –HORACE

For twelve long years imprisoned and persecuted for religious reasons, John Bunyan's lips were silenced in Bedford jail. It was there, however, that he did his greatest and best work of his life, for there he wrote the book that has been read most next to the Bible, *Pilgrim's Progress*.[1]

It is generally accepted that Paul's Roman incarceration produced three great letters to the churches of Ephesus, Colosse, and Philippi, as well as a personal letter to his friend Philemon.

While the prison epistles reflect Paul's earthly position as a prisoner of Rome, he makes it clear that his captivity was first and foremost to Christ. . . . Paul's time in prison was for the purpose of the spreading of the gospel in the Gentile capital of Rome. The Lord Himself told Paul to "take courage! As you have testified about me in Jerusalem, so you must also testify in Rome" (Acts 23:11). Paul's time in captivity was no less profitable to us today than it was to the first-century churches he loved so well.[2]

Dr. Hubert Davidson visited the noted poetess, Myra Brooks Welch, who perhaps is best known for her masterpiece, "The Touch of the Master's Hand." As he turned to leave her home, Myra patted the arm of her wheelchair and said, "And I thank God for this.'"

Imagine being thankful for a wheelchair! But her talent lay undiscovered before her wheelchair days. Rather than becoming bitter, she chose a better way, and a wonderful ministry opened new doors of blessings for her. Her poems have blessed the whole world.[3]

A farmer caught a young eagle and placed it with his chickens. The eaglet ate with them and soon adapted itself to their ways. One day a naturalist visited the farmer. Seeing the eaglet, he said, "That's not a chicken! That's an eagle!" "That's right," said the farmer, "but he's no longer an eagle in his nature. He's a chicken now, for he eats chicken food and does everything chickens do. He will never fly again!"

"You're wrong," said the naturalist. "He's an eagle still, because he has the heart of an eagle." After making several unsuccessful attempts to get the eagle to fly, he took it to the foot of a high mountain just as the sun was rising. The minute the eagle got a glimpse of the rising sun, he uttered a wild scream of joy, stretched his wings and mounted higher and higher into the sky, never to return to the farmer.[4]

People who have the heart of an eagle are those who rise above that which could be disastrous for them, who think on the goodness of the Lord, even when much is going wrong, and who are grateful for His mercy and care, knowing and understanding Lamentations 3:22: "It is of the LORD's mercies that we are not consumed, because his compassions fail not."

You, child of God, have an eagle's heart. You were meant to fly high, to be set free, and to live with your eyes focused on the Savior of the world, keeping Him in your vision at all times!

"But unto you that fear my name shall the Sun of righteousness arise with healing in his wings" (Malachi 4:2).

Note, the devil, though he is an enemy to all saints, is a conquered enemy. The Captain of our salvation has defeated and disarmed him; we have nothing to do but to pursue the victory.
–Matthew Henry[5]

4
CHASTISED

*To suffer for one's own faults – ah! –
there is the sting of life.*
–Oscar Wilde[1]

Psalm 106 describes in a nutshell God's dealings with the children of Israel from the deliverance out of Egypt through the wilderness. "Many times did he deliver them; but they provoked him with their counsel, and were brought low for their iniquity" (Psalm 106:43). When they humbled themselves and cried out to God, He was merciful to their cries, "Nevertheless he regarded their affliction, when he heard their cry: and he remembered for them his covenant, and repented according to the multitude of his mercies" (Psalm 106:44–45).

THANK GOD FOR PAIN!

No tear hath ever yet been shed in vain,
And in the end each sorrowing heart shall find
No curse, but blessings in the hand of pain;
Even when he smiteth, then is God most kind.

Thank God for pain!
–AUTHOR UNKNOWN

Blessed is the man whom thou chastenest, O LORD, and teachest him out of thy law.
(Psalm 94:12)

My son, despise not thou the chastening of the
Lord, nor faint when thou art rebuked of him: for
whom the Lord loveth he chasteneth, and scour-
geth every son whom he receiveth. If ye endure
chastening, God dealeth with you as with sons;
for what son is he whom the father chasteneth
not? But if ye be without chastisement, whereof
all are partakers, then are ye bastards, and not
sons. . . . Now no chastening for the present
seemeth to be joyous, but grievous: nevertheless
afterward it yieldeth the peaceable fruit of righteousness unto them which are exercised thereby.
(Hebrews 12:5–8, 11)

JONAH

One of the great examples of God's chastisement is Jonah.
The word of the Lord came to Jonah and told him, "Arise,

go to Nineveh, that great city, and cry against it; for their wickedness is come up before me." Jonah in his ignorance thought he could run from the call of God. But Jonah fled "from the presence of the LORD." (See Jonah 1:2-3.)

It's so strange that people think they can hide from their Creator, the omnipresent God, who knows all things and sees all things. God was watching Jonah the whole time he was trying to mingle with the crowd and disappear. So God, who controls the wind, just spoke and told the wind to create a mighty tempest in the sea where Jonah was hiding in the ship.

The wind whipped and started blowing up a storm, so much that it looked like the ship was going to be blown to pieces. All the mariners were afraid and calling out to their gods, while throwing the ship's wares over the side to lighten the load. Meanwhile Jonah was asleep below until the captain of the ship woke him up, saying, "What meanest thou, O sleeper? arise, call upon thy God, if so be that God will think upon us, that we perish not." The crew said, "Let us cast lots, that we may know for whose cause this evil is upon us. So they cast lots, and the lot fell upon Jonah" (Jonah 1:6-7). Then they asked him to tell them who he was and where he was from; they wanted to know why the evil was come upon them. It must have been an unusual storm for them to know it wasn't a normal storm.

Jonah told them he was a Hebrew and that he feared the Lord God of Heaven, the same God who had created the sea and the dry land. Then the men were even more frightened and asked Jonah what they should do to him so the sea would be calm again. He told them to throw him overboard. He would rather die than preach to the Ninevites.

YOU CAN RUN FROM GOD, BUT YOU CAN'T OUTRUN HIM!

You can run from God, but you can't outrun Him! Jonah was never out from under the eye of God. The beautiful part about this story is that God went after Jonah. David talks about chasing after God, but here we have God chasing a man. It is mercy personified! God knew the people of Nineveh were going to repent, but they needed a preacher to preach to them. God chose an arrogant prophet to fill those shoes. The audacity of Jonah to think he could hide from God and renege on the call!

Actually, mercy brought everything together. God is the great Potentate, the One who rules the universe, yet He was concerned about one man and one wicked city.

God wasn't going to let Jonah die, but He was going to chastise him so he would cry out for mercy. He prepared a large fish to swallow Jonah, who was in the creature's belly three days and three nights.

The man who went into the fish was totally different from the man who came out. Jonah described his horrible three days and nights of being brought low, how he went to the bottom of the mountains:

1. An affliction
2. Belly of hell
3. Cast into the deep
4. Floods, billows, waves compassed me
5. [Dark] waters surrounding me
6. [Slimy] weeds wrapped around my head

7.   The earth with [prison] bars around me

This all made him cry to the Lord. "When my soul fainted within me I remembered the LORD: and my prayer came in unto thee, into thine holy temple. . . . But I will sacrifice unto thee with the voice of thanksgiving; I will pay that that I have vowed. Salvation is of the LORD" (Jonah 2:7, 9).

When Jonah was brought low, his stubborn arrogance left and was replaced by repenting and begging for his life. That's when God spoke to the fish to vomit Jonah onto dry land. Jonah gratefully picked himself up and went to preach to the heathen city that God was going to destroy them.

> It is a great mercy to be reclaimed and called home when we go astray, though it be by a tempest. –MATTHEW HENRY[2]

DAVID

Psalm 94:12–13 pronounces a blessing on those God chastises: "Blessed is the man whom thou chastenest, O LORD, and teachest him out of thy law; that thou mayest give him rest from the days of adversity." Although David sinned greatly, God loved him more greatly because of his humble heart in response to correction.

We've already addressed the three major sins of David, which caused God great displeasure. Several of his psalms echo the pain he felt when he was chastised. Psalm 38, in particular, reflects David's suffering: "I am feeble and sore broken: I have roared by reason of the disquietness of my heart" (Psalm 38:8); "my heart panteth, my strength faileth me" (Psalm 38:10). Psalm 51 in its entirety recounts the effects of David's sin on his life.

God did not let David down. His mercy encompassed him, and He restored his joy. Yet sometimes we chastise ourselves without realizing it. It's one thing for God to bring us low, but it's another thing for our mouths to bring us low. This happened to a man in the Bible who made a foolish and rash vow.

JEPHTHAH

Jephthah, the judge of Israel, was asked by the elders of Gilead to help them fight against the children of Ammon. He said he would do it if they made him their head. They agreed, and he made a vow to God, "If thou shalt without fail deliver the children of Ammon into mine hands, then it shall be, that whatsoever cometh forth of the doors of my house to meet me, when I return in peace from the children of Ammon, shall surely be the LORD's, and I will offer it up for a burnt offering" (Judges 11:30–31).

"When Jephthah returned to his home in Mizpah, who should come out to meet him but his daughter, dancing to the sound of timbrels! She was an only child. Except for her he had neither son nor daughter" (Judges 11:34, NIV). "And it came to pass, when he saw her, that he rent his clothes, and said, Alas, my daughter! thou hast brought me very low, and thou art one of them that trouble me: for I have opened my mouth unto the LORD, and I cannot go back" (Judges 11:35).

There are different viewpoints on what really happened with the vow, but I prefer to think *Gill's Exposition on the Entire Bible* is correct: "What he had to do was to repent of this rash vow, and humble himself before God for making it, and not add sin to sin by performing it."[3]

Words have been around from the beginning of time. In the beginning God created the world by *speaking* to it. The phrase, "and God said" is used nine times in Genesis 1. "And God said, Let there be light: and there was light."

Jesus spoke to the demons. He spoke to the winds. He spoke to spirits of infirmity, and He spoke to dead people: "Lazarus come forth!"

He told us to speak to our mountains.

A leading neurosurgeon once said to Dr. Cho, "Did you know that the speech center in the brain rules over all the nerves? According to our recent findings in neurology, the speech center in the brain has total dominion over all the other nerves." He said that the speech nerve center had such power over all the body that simply speaking can give one control over his body to manipulate it in the way he wishes. He said, "If someone keeps saying, 'I'm going to become weak,' then right away all the nerves receive that message and they say, 'Oh, let's prepare to become weak, for we've received instructions from our central communication that we should become weak.'"[4]

HE TOLD US TO SPEAK TO OUR MOUNTAINS.

Words start wars, can cause death or can speak life: "Death and life are in the power of the tongue" (Proverbs 18:21). "Whoso that keepeth his mouth and his tongue keepeth his soul from troubles" (Proverbs 21:23). God hears every word that is spoken.

But I say unto you, That every idle word that men shall speak, they shall give account thereof in the day of judgment. For by thy words thou shalt be justified, and by thy words thou shalt be condemned. (Matthew 12:36–37)

We must be careful of what we say. Let us not talk ourselves into trouble that brings us low but pray daily, "Let the words of my mouth, and the meditation of my heart, be acceptable in thy sight, O LORD, my strength, and my redeemer" (Psalm 19:14).

In closing this chapter, God didn't chastise the apostle Paul in the following passage, but He did allow Satan to buffet him with a thorn in his flesh:

For though I would desire to glory, I shall not be a fool; for I will say the truth: but now I forbear, lest any man should think of me above that which he seeth me to be, or that he heareth of me. And lest I should be exalted above measure through the abundance of the revelations, there was given to me a thorn in the flesh, the messenger of Satan to buffet me, lest I should be exalted above measure. For this thing I besought the Lord thrice, that it might depart from me. And he said unto me, My grace is sufficient for thee: for my strength is made perfect in weakness. Most gladly therefore will I rather glory in my infirmities, that the power of Christ may rest upon me. (II Corinthians 12:6–9)

What a powerful attitude! That's why Paul could write under the anointing these words of victory, "We are troubled on every side, yet not distressed; we are perplexed, but not in despair; persecuted, but not forsaken; cast down, but not destroyed; always bearing about in the body the dying of the Lord Jesus, that the life also of Jesus might be made manifest in our body" (II Corinthians 4:8–10).

5
PROVED AND MADE TO PROSPER

"In the darkest night to be certain of the dawn . . .
to go through Hell and to continue to trust in the
goodness of God — this is the challenge
and the way."
Abraham Joshua Heschel[1]

There was a man in the land of Uz, whose name was Job; and that man was perfect and upright, and one that feared God, and eschewed evil. . . . Now there was a day when the sons of God came to present themselves before the LORD, and Satan came also among them. And the LORD said unto Satan, Whence comest thou? Then Satan answered the LORD, and said, From going to and fro in the earth, and from walking up and down in it. And the LORD said unto Satan, Hast thou

81

considered my servant Job, that there is none like him in the earth, a perfect and an upright man, one that feareth God, and escheweth evil? Then Satan answered the LORD, and said, Doth Job fear God for nought? Hast not thou made an hedge about him, and about his house, and about all that he hath on every side? thou hast blessed the work of his hands, and his substance is increased in the land. But put forth thine hand now, and touch all that he hath, and he will curse thee to thy face. And the LORD said unto Satan, Behold, all that he hath is in thy power; only upon himself put not forth thine hand. So Satan went forth from the presence of the LORD. (Job 1:1, 6–12)

Job passed the test and didn't even know he was the subject of conversation between God and the devil; if only Job would have known! He felt like God was against him when he said, "Have pity upon me, have pity upon me, O ye my friends; for the hand of God hath touched me" (Job 19:21). It wasn't God who had done the evil, but He did allow Satan to do it, knowing that Job would not fail Him.

I marvel at Job. In one verse he felt sorry that he had been brought low; then within a few verses he said with faith, "For I know that my redeemer liveth, and that he shall stand at the latter day upon the earth: and though after my skin worms destroy this body, yet in my flesh shall I see God" (Job 19:25–26).

Job was brought low before God raised him up. As the psalmist wrote, "Thou, which hast shewed me great and sore troubles, shalt quicken me again, and shalt bring me up again from the depths of the earth" (Psalm 71:20).

Job cried rivers of tears, so much that he said: "My face is foul with weeping, and on my eyelids is the shadow of death" (Job 16:16). Yet Job did nothing wrong! He was a righteous man, and God was so sure of Job's allegiance to Him that He taunted Satan, using Job as bait. Sure enough, when all Satan's attacks came against him and after Job had lost everything, "then Job arose, and rent his mantle, and shaved his head, and fell down upon the ground, and worshipped, and said, Naked came I out of my mother's womb, and naked shall I return thither: the LORD gave, and the LORD hath taken away; blessed be the name of the LORD" (Job 1:20–21).

> WHEN BAD THINGS HAPPEN TO YOU, YOU NEVER KNOW WHAT'S GOING ON IN THE UNSEEN WORLD.

Job proved himself worthy of God's confidence in him.

As the trial intensified with his best friends calling him a liar and a hypocrite, Job uttered those famous words that have been quoted through the ages, "Though he slay me, yet will I trust in him: but I will maintain mine own ways before him" (Job 13:15).

When bad things happen to you, you never know what's going on in the unseen world. God might be showing you off to Satan, confident of your love and worship to Him. That's why it's imperative to let the Word of God dwell in you richly. (See Colossians 3:16.) We don't want to let God down.

It wasn't easy for Job. He was as human as everyone else and expressed the pain he felt in Job 6:4: "For the arrows of the Almighty are within me, the poison whereof drinketh up my spirit: the terrors of God do set themselves in array against me."

Job loved and revered his God and was perfect in the sight of God. Even though he lost everything, even though his friends attacked his character and accused him falsely; he never lost his true character—his unwavering faith in God. The following poem describes the disloyalty of Job's friends:

> Fame is vapor;
> Popularity is an accident.
> Riches take wings and fly.
> Those who cheer you today
> May curse you and stab you tomorrow.
> Then there is only one thing left—
> That is: CHARACTER.
> — HORACE GREELEY[2]

This is what happened to Job. His three trusted friends came to him and just stared at him. When they began to talk, they did not encourage him but accused him of sins they thought he had committed.

Job was a perfect man, who served God and did everything right; he did not deserve what happened to him. He could have become offended and bitter toward God, but he didn't. Although he did have lots of questions and laments, he never lost his faith in God.

In June 2016, during my time of healing and waiting on God to restore me to full health, I was awakened during the wee hours of the morning. I began to pray because I didn't feel well, and I didn't want to wake the girls to pray with me. I couldn't understand why it was taking so long to get my strength back and asked God for the reason behind several things. While I prayed, with tears dripping on my pillow, the story of John the Baptist came to me. John sent word to Jesus and asked, "Should we look for another?" And Jesus answered him, "Blessed is he who is not offended in me."

Several times through the years, God has shown me truths in connection with this verse, "Blessed is he, whosoever shall not be offended in me" (Luke 7:23). I remember when I first heard my late husband, Kenneth Haney, preach on this. He said Josephus wrote about this and said it meant, "Blessed is he who is not offended how I do My business."

As I thought on it, I could understand why John felt like he did. He knew Jesus had the power to get him out of prison, and why wasn't He doing it if He was who He said He was?

Early the next morning, my daughter Stephenie came into my room. (She had flown home to be with me to help Angela and stayed about three weeks.) She reminded me recently of that special morning and sent me the following memory in a text:

> It was one of the mornings when I went into her room to sit beside her, and she told me that God had given her a word. Through the night she had

a few scary moments that we called "episodes" as she was dealing with the aftermath of the strokes. But she didn't awaken me or my sister Angela this time. That particular early morning, she told me she was praying and asking God why wouldn't He take these symptoms away, that she wanted it to be over so she could move on. She started crying as she told me His response.

He told her, "Blessed is he who is not offended in me." Then He took her to the story about John the Baptist. It resonated with me, and I tucked that golden nugget deep inside my heart.

Today as I deal with issues that are outside of my control, I find myself going back to that morning, where I was sitting by my mother and listening to her tell me how the Lord had spoken to her. It calmed her even though a dark cloud had been lingering over her through the night.

During this long trial God allowed me to go through, I said over and over, "As for God, His ways are perfect!" found in the song of deliverance sang by David: "As for God, his way is perfect; the word of the LORD is tried: he is a buckler to all them that trust in him" (II Samuel 22:31).

You can get weary during a low time, but don't let weariness win. Famous words by the renowned boxer James Corbett apply to the spiritual journey when you've been brought low:

Fight one more round. When your feet are so tired that you have to shuffle back to the centre of the ring, fight one more round. When your arms are so tired that you can hardly lift your hands to come on guard, fight one more round. When your nose is bleeding and your eyes are black and you are so tired you wish your opponent would crack you one on the jaw and put you to sleep, fight one more round—remembering that the man who always fights one more round is never whipped.

Sir Winston Churchill said it this way: "If you're going through hell, keep going!" Paul wrote, "Fight the good fight of faith" (I Timothy 6:12). When the enemy says, "It's over!" pick up your feet and trudge on in

GOD'S PROMISES HAVE NO EXPIRATION DATE.

spite of pain and struggle. It's no time to give in to defeat. God is with you, and He is telling you to press on to victory.

You *will* get through the desert of pain. The trial won't last forever. Keep your hand in the Master's hand, for He invited, "Come to me, all who are weary and burdened, and I will give you rest" (Matthew 11:28, NIV). Just tell the enemy, "Rejoice not against me, O mine enemy: when I fall, I shall arise; when I sit in darkness, the LORD shall be a light unto me" (Micah 7:8).

Remind yourself, God's promises have no expiration date. If He said it, it will happen. David said, "I had fainted, unless I had believed to see the goodness of the LORD in the land of the living. Wait on the LORD: be of good courage, and he shall strengthen thine heart: wait, I say, on the LORD" (Psalm 27:13–14). Even when it looks like nothing's happening, God watches, waits, and moves in His time.

At the end of Job's trial, he prayed a prayer of humility. "I abhor myself, and repent in dust and ashes" (Job 42:6). "And the LORD turned the captivity of Job, when he prayed for his friends: also the LORD gave Job twice as much as he had before" (Job 42:10). His friends were those who had accused him falsely and didn't treat him right. He didn't harbor ill-will or resentment in his heart toward them, for his desire to be delivered was greater than the pain they had caused. Not only did God give Job double back, but He reprimanded Job's friends and made them offer a sacrifice and repent. He instructed them to have Job pray for them.

> God *turned his captivity*, that is, he redressed his grievances and took away all the causes of his complaints; he loosed him from the bond with which Satan had now, for a great while, bound him, and delivered him out of those cruel hands into which He had delivered him.
>
> We may suppose that now all his bodily pains and distempers were healed so suddenly and so thoroughly that the cure was next to miraculous: *His flesh became fresher than a child's, and he returned to the days of his youth;* and, what was more, he felt a very great alteration in his mind; it was calm and easy, and the tumult was all over, his disquieting thoughts had all vanished, his fears were silenced, and the consolations of God were now as much the delight of his soul as his terrors had been his burdens.[3]

One minute, Job was sitting on a pile of ashes, scraping his boils, then crying out to God in repentance, and after Eliphaz offered a sacrifice for Job, God turned his captivity. The next thing we see is Job in his house receiving his sisters, brothers, friends, and the gifts they brought him. It was truly a miraculous deliverance!

> Extraordinary afflictions are not always the punishment of extraordinary sins, but sometimes the trial of extraordinary graces.
> –MATTHEW HENRY[4]

6
FOR HIS KINGDOM'S SAKE

The only significance of life consists in helping to establish the kingdom of God.
–Leo Tolstoy

> Our Father which art in heaven, Hallowed be thy name. Thy kingdom come. Thy will be done in earth, as it is in heaven. . . . For thine is the kingdom, and the power, and the glory, for ever. Amen. (Matthew 6:9–10, 13)

"Hast thou not known" is the message of Heaven. "Hast thou not known? hast thou not heard, that the everlasting God, the LORD, the Creator of the ends of the earth, fainteth not, neither is weary? there is no searching of his understanding" (Isaiah 40:28). All we do on earth should bring glory to the only true, majestic God.

> Many people would not kill a mouse without publishing it. Samson killed a lion and said nothing about it. Say much of what the Lord has done for you. Say little of what you have done for the Lord. Do not speak a self-glorifying sentence.
> –SPURGEON[1]

I wonder how many people would be as fervent about furthering God's kingdom in the earth if their name remained anonymous? Are we racing or competing with each other or racing eternity? So much remains for us to do for God's kingdom. God, give us kingdom eyes to see as You see, to see You and Your vision. Thy kingdom come!

Do not rely on people to validate you. Only God can give you the validation that you need. If you depend on people to validate you, you will be disappointed. It should not matter if you are never recognized for what you do; people are fickle, but God is constant. Seeking His favor and approval should be the highest goal in life.

JEREMIAH

God needed a man who was selfless, given only to God, because the sins of the people had separated them from God. Jeremiah would become God's mouthpiece, and he would be brought low because of the truth for which he stood. Before all this happened, however, Jeremiah and God had a conversation. God spoke first,

> Before I formed thee in the belly I knew thee; and before thou camest forth out of the womb I sanctified thee, and I ordained thee a prophet unto

the nations. Then said I, Ah, Lord GOD! behold, I cannot speak: for I am a child. But the LORD said unto me, Say not, I am a child: for thou shalt go to all that I shall send thee, and whatsoever I command thee thou shalt speak. Be not afraid of their faces: for I am with thee to deliver thee, saith the LORD. Then the LORD put forth his hand, and touched my mouth. And the LORD said unto me, Behold, I have put my words in thy mouth. See, I have this day set thee over the nations and over the kingdoms, to root out, and to pull down, and to destroy, and to throw down, to build, and to plant. (Jeremiah 1:5–10)

God laid out His plan for Jeremiah:
- To root out
- To pull down
- To destroy
- To throw down
- To build
- To plant

God was concerned because His people were following other gods. He said to Jeremiah, "I will utter my judgments against them touching all their wickedness, who have forsaken me, and have burned incense unto other gods, and worshipped the works of their own hands" (Jeremiah 1:16).

Then God spoke to Jeremiah words of power and reassurance: "I have made thee this day a defenced city, and an iron pillar, and brasen walls against the whole land, against the kings of Judah, against the princes thereof, against the priests thereof, and against the people of the land" (Jeremiah 1:18).

God had confidence in Jeremiah and described him as:
- A defensed city
- An iron pillar
- Brazen walls

God had a purpose for Jeremiah's life before he was even born. He would face difficulties, opposition, imprisonment, and anger from the leaders and people of the land to whom he would prophesy, but He was not alone. God said, "And they shall fight against thee; but they shall not prevail against thee; for I am with thee, saith the LORD, to deliver thee" (Jeremiah 1:19).

Jeremiah's first message was to the backslidden people of Jerusalem. God told him to cry in their ears. Jeremiah began to preach to them and gave them the message God gave him: "For my people have committed two evils; they have forsaken me the fountain of living waters, and hewed them out cisterns, broken cisterns, that can hold no water" (Jeremiah 2:13).

Then God, through Jeremiah, described what was happening: "O generation, see ye the word of the LORD. Have I been a wilderness unto Israel? a land of darkness? wherefore say my people, We are lords; we will come no more unto thee? Can a maid forget her ornaments, or a bride her attire? yet my people have forgotten me days without number" (Jeremiah 2:31-32).

Then it came: his first persecution! Jeremiah stood in the court of the Lord's house and said to all the people: "Thus saith the LORD of hosts, the God of Israel; Behold,

I will bring upon this city and upon all her towns all the evil that I have pronounced against it, because they have hardened their necks, that they might not hear my words" (Jeremiah 19:15).

When Pashur the son of Immer the priest, who also served as the chief governor in the house of the Lord, heard that Jeremiah prophesied those things, it angered him. "Then Pashur smote Jeremiah the prophet, and put him in the stocks that were in the high gate of Benjamin, which was by the house of the LORD" (Jeremiah 20:2).

When they released Jeremiah from the stocks, he just kept preaching because he was on a mission as the spokesman for God. He angered the leaders, and together they plotted against him until they cried to the king, "We beseech thee, let this man be put to death! . . . Then Zedekiah the king said, Behold, he is in your hand: for the king is not he that can do anything against you. Then took they Jeremiah, and cast him into the dungeon . . . and they let down Jeremiah with cords. And in the dungeon there was no water, but mire: so Jeremiah sunk in the mire" (Jeremiah 38:4–6).

Ebed-melech the Ethiopian, one of the eunuchs in the king's house, heard they had put Jeremiah in prison, so he went to the king and told him that Jeremiah would die in the pit without any food. He asked permission to pull him out of the dungeon, which the king granted him. Jeremiah was brought out of the dungeon but kept in chains in the prison courtyard.

Jeremiah described his experiences: "Mine enemies chased me sore, like a bird, without cause. They have cut off my life in the dungeon, and cast a stone upon me.

Waters flowed over mind head; then I said, I am cut off. I called upon thy name, O LORD, out of the low dungeon" (Lamentations 3:52–55).

Dark places, hedges, heavy chains, no idea where God was, desolation, object of jokes, target of the enemy, bitter trials, ashes for a covering, affliction, gall: these were the experiences that went with the job description God had chosen for Jeremiah before he was born. God trusted Jeremiah with a job nobody would apply for in modern times. Who wants to be put into a dungeon, hated, and made into a buffoon?

At times he cried, "Cursed be the day wherein I was born! . . . Wherefore came I forth out of the womb to see labour and sorrow, that my days should be consumed with shame?" (Jeremiah 20:14, 18).

But after all Jeremiah's lamenting, he realized that without God He would be dead anyway and wrote words of hope which have been quoted innumerable times:

> It is of the LORD's mercies that we are not con-sumed, because his compassions fail not. They are new every morning: great is thy faithfulness. The LORD is my portion, saith my soul; therefore will I hope in him. The LORD is good unto them that wait for him, to the soul that seeketh him. (Lamentations 3:22–25)

People generally want accolades, approval, favor from people, and a life in nice surroundings. Being in God's ser-vice is not always bright lights and applause. Sometimes it involves being brought low, sinking in situations beyond your control, without much hope in sight. No matter where life places you, you are under God's watchful eye, and He is with you each step of the way. Just as the king commanded men to lift Jeremiah from the mire, God lifts us into a place of safety.

JESUS

Jesus told His disciples in the Garden of Gethsemane: "My soul is exceeding sorrowful, even unto death: tarry ye here, and watch with me" (Matthew 26:38). Then He went a little further and prayed: "O my Father, if it be possible,

NO MATTER WHERE LIFE PLACES YOU, GOD IS WITH YOU EACH STEP OF THE WAY.

let this cup pass from me: nevertheless not as I will, but as thou wilt" (Matthew 26:39). Even though Jesus knew His flesh would feel horrible pain, the sinless Christ endured humiliation and degradation so a world could be set free from the chains and bondage of sin. He was:
1. Wounded
2. Stripped
3. Rejected
4. Misunderstood
5. Falsely Accused
6. Envied
7. Forsaken
8. Crucified

But on the third day He rose from the dead and now reigns in Heaven as Lord of lords and King of kings forevermore. He is the great I Am, the almighty God, who appeared to Abraham in the Old Testament: "And when Abram was ninety years old and nine, the LORD appeared to Abram, and said unto him, I am the Almighty God; walk before me, and be thou perfect" (Genesis 17:1). He confirmed His identity in Revelation 1:8, 18: "I am Alpha and Omega, the beginning and the ending, saith the Lord, which is, and which was, and which is to come, the Almighty. . . . I am he that liveth, and was dead; and, behold, I am alive for evermore, Amen; and have the keys of hell and of death."

PAUL

God's ministers are servants who look at the Cross and are challenged to give their very life for the gospel's sake, no matter the cost.

One of these was Paul the apostle, who was brought low often, as he said in Philippians 4:12: "I know also how to be brought low, and I know how to abound. In everything, and in all things, I have learned the secret also to be full and to hunger, also to abound and to be deficient" (Berean Literal Bible).

God had a reason for it all. He needed a jailer converted, so He allowed Paul and Silas's backs to be beaten.

Paul described his low points at length in the following passage of Scripture:

> Are they ministers of Christ? (I speak as a fool) I am more; in labours more abundant, in stripes above measure, in prisons more frequent, in deaths oft. Of the Jews five times received I

forty stripes save one. Thrice was I beaten with rods, once was I stoned, thrice I suffered shipwreck, a night and a day I have been in the deep; in journeyings often, in perils of waters, in perils of robbers, in perils by mine own countrymen, in perils by the heathen, in perils in the city, in perils in the wilderness, in perils in the sea, in perils among false brethren; in weariness and painfulness, in watchings often, in hunger and thirst, in fastings often, in cold and nakedness. Beside those things that are without, that which cometh upon me daily, the care of all the churches." (II Corinthians 11:23–28)

Yet in it all, he was an overcomer. He thundered:

Who shall separate us from the love of Christ? shall tribulation, or distress, or persecution, or famine, or nakedness, or peril, or sword? As it is written, For thy sake we are killed all the day long; we are accounted as sheep for the slaughter. Nay, in all these things we are more than conquerors through him that loved us. For I am persuaded, that neither death, nor life, nor angels, nor principalities, nor powers, nor things present, nor things to come, nor height, nor depth, nor any other creature, shall be able to separate us from the love of God, which is in Christ Jesus our Lord. (Romans 8:35–39)

Prison did not stop him from preaching. He wrote many of the epistles while imprisoned for the sake of the gospel. He was not afraid or hindered from what God called him to do on that miraculous encounter he had with the Lord Jesus on the Damascus road.

> And now, compelled by the Spirit, I am going to Jerusalem, not knowing what will happen to me there. I only know that in every city the Holy Spirit warns me that prison and hardships are facing me. (Acts 20:22–23, NIV)

> But none of these things move me, neither count I my life dear unto myself, so that I might finish my course with joy, and the ministry, which I have received of the Lord Jesus, to testify the gospel of the grace of God. (Acts 20:24, KJV)

There have been many martyrs for the kingdom's sake through the ages. All the disciples gave their lives and were martyred for truth (except for John, and they tried to kill him too). Another martyr for the kingdom's sake was a Bible translator.

> More than five hundred years ago, it was a crime to own a Bible in English. The ban was broken by a few courageous men of God whose eyes were open to the need of the people for a Bible they could read. One of the greatest of this little company of heroes was William Tyndale. He was forced to leave his native England, never to

return. Working in Europe, he labored long years to translate the Bible into English. He printed the first English New Testament in 1525.

Tyndale wrote tracts and encouraged the people to read the Bible. One such tract was as follows: "Let it not make thee despair, neither yet discourage thee, O reader, that it is forbidden thee in pain of life and goods, or that it is made breaking of the king's peace, or treason unto his highness, to read the Word of thy soul's health — for if God be on our side, what matter maketh it who be against us, be they bishops, cardinals, popes."

Finally, in early August 1536, Tyndale was condemned as a heretic, degraded from the priesthood, and delivered to the secular authorities for punishment. On Friday, October 6, after local officials took their seats, Tyndale was brought to the cross in the middle of the town square and given a chance to recant. That refused, he was given a moment to pray. English historian John Foxe said he cried out, "Lord, open the King of England's eyes!"

Then he was bound to the beam, and both an iron chain and a rope were put around his neck. Gunpowder was added to the brush and logs. At the signal of a local official, the executioner, standing behind Tyndale, quickly tightened the noose, strangling him. Then an official took up a lighted torch and handed it to the executioner, who set the wood ablaze.[2]

No matter the heinous crimes against those who loved the Bible by men who were evil and despised good, God always gets the last word, and someday the perpetrators will suffer worse punishment than what they inflicted upon their victims. God takes care of His own, and He will reward the faithful soldiers of the cross.

The following story is told about the troopship *Birkenhead*:

> In 1852 the troopship *Birkenhead* struck on a sunken rock off the African coast: she had on board drafts of the 12th Lancers and other regiments, with 124 women and children. They were the ones who got into the boats, while the men, drawn up by their officers as on parade, saw without a murmur the boats shove off, and went down with the sinking ship.
>
> The word of command was given by Major Seton, "Stand still, and die like Englishmen;" and those four hundred and fifty-four men went down to their sea-grave that day in soldierly order, firm, and steady, since there was only room in the boats for the women and children.[3]

First Corinthians 15:58 gives the command from Heaven to its soldiers: "Therefore, my beloved brethren, be ye stedfast, unmoveable, always abounding in the work of the Lord, forasmuch as ye know that your labour is not in vain in the Lord." We find a similar order in II Timothy 2:3–4: "Thou therefore endure hardness, as a good soldier of Jesus Christ. No man that warreth entangleth himself with the affairs of this life; that he may please him who hath chosen him to be a soldier."

No matter what path God leads you down for His kingdom's sake, it will be, as the old song goes, worth it all when we see Jesus. When He asks us to do something for His name's sake that we would rather not do, we will do it for His kingdom's sake, no matter how difficult it is to do. I will be brave and remember that,

> For every hill I've had to climb,
> For every stone that bruised my feet,
> For all the blood and sweat and grime,
> For blinding storms and burning heat
> My heart sings but a grateful song;
> These were the things that made me strong!
>
> For all the heartaches and the tears,
> For all the anguish and the pain,
> For gloomy days and fruitless years,
> And for the hopes that lived in vain,
> I do give thanks, for now I know
> These were the things that helped me grow!
>
> 'Tis not the softer things of life
> Which stimulate one's will to strive;
> But bleak adversity and strife
> Do most to keep one's will alive,
> O'er rose-strewn paths the weaklings creep,
> But brave hearts dare to climb the steep.[4]

CHAPTER 6

I woke up early the morning of May 1, 2018, saying these words: "The sufferings are not worthy to be compared to the glory." It was going over and over in my mind. I said, "Yes, Lord, You want it in the book again, but where?" This is where I felt He wanted it: "For I reckon that the sufferings of this present time are not worthy to be compared with the glory which shall be revealed in us" (Romans 8:18).

Strong faith is often exercised with strong trials.

–MATTHEW HENRY[5]

7

PREPARE FOR GREATER WORK

Noble souls, through dust and heat,
Rise from disaster and defeat
The stronger.
–Henry Wadsworth Longfellow[1]

My lowliness is my loftiness, my loftiness my lowliness.[2]

THE WAY UP IS DOWN

In London, 637 steps lead into the beautiful dome of St. Paul's Cathedral. About nine-tenths of the way up, just at the base of the dome, an exit brings one outside, onto a promenade with a marvelous view of the city. To climb up to the apex of the dome, one has to return to the interior through a small door on which there is a sign that reads, "Go down, to go up."

Just as one must go down to go up to see the dome, many times this same element of truth is essential in reaching a goal or realizing a dream. This was true in the life of a handsome young lad named Joseph.

When Joseph was young, the Lord gave him a dream, and from that dream the plan for Joseph's life began to unfold. He was the favored son of Jacob, his father, and was given a special coat of many colors to signify this. One day he was wandering through the mountains trying to find his brothers when a man asked him where he was going. The young man told him he was trying to find his brothers, who were with their flocks. The man told him to go to Dothan, and he would find them there. As Joseph neared their camp, he was entering the first part of the long road toward the fulfillment of his dream. "And when they saw him afar off, even before he came near unto them, they conspired against him to slay him. And they said one to another, Behold, this dreamer cometh" (Genesis 37:18–19).

The circumstances following his misfortunate appearance made it seem as if God had forgotten Joseph and his dream. First, instead of his brothers welcoming him, they threw him into a pit while they decided whether to kill him. Sometimes you are placed in a situation that is desolate and bare; no life-giving water or hope is there, only emptiness and solitude. But God was watching the whole scenario.

The Lord knew the thirteen-year bizarre trial was necessary to prepare Joseph for the throne of leadership he would occupy. It seemed as if Joseph was alone, but in reality, he was beginning his ascent toward what God had planned for him. God did not let Joseph down, but neither did Joseph let God down. He never cursed God or accused Him of being unfair, but Joseph remained faithful to God in every situation God allowed him to experience.

Then because of Judah's reasoning, Joseph's brothers roughly hauled him out of the pit and sold him to a band of traveling Ishmaelites. Imagine a young lad thrown in with a group of people he had never met, with strange customs and without belief in his God. After loneliness, isolation from family, and a brutal trip through the desert, the merchants sold him as a slave to a man named Potiphar, an officer of Pharaoh.

The heart of Joseph was filled with pain from the hate he had received from his brothers. He was now under the ownership of a man who did not serve his God. However, while everything appeared to be negative, he was still in God's plan.

> And the LORD was with Joseph, and he was a prosperous man; and he was in the house of his master the Egyptian. And his master saw that the LORD was with him, and that the LORD made all that he did to prosper in his hand. And Joseph found grace in his sight, and he served him: and he made him overseer over his house, and all that he had he put into his hand. And it came to pass from the time that he had made him overseer in his house, and over all that he had, that the LORD blessed the Egyptian's house for Joseph's sake; and the blessing of the LORD was upon all that he had in the house, and in the field. (Genesis 39:2–5)

Genesis 39:6 describes Joseph well. It says, "And Joseph was a goodly person, and well favoured."

Even though Joseph had come through his first trial without losing his grip on things, more things would test him before his dream came to pass. The Scripture says that Potiphar's wife cast her eyes upon Joseph, and she tried to seduce him to lie with her. Joseph's integrity with God would not let him do this sinful thing. You would think that, because he did the right thing, everything would turn out all right, but it did not.

Potiphar's wife was persistent in her flirtations with Joseph. Day after day she tried to get him to sin with her. He always said no, but the day came when he went into the house and no one was inside but her.

> And she caught him by his garment, saying, Lie with me: and he left his garment in her hand, and fled, and got him out. And it came to pass, when she saw that he had left his garment in her hand, and was fled forth, that she called unto the men of her house, and spake unto them, saying, See, he hath brought in an Hebrew unto us to mock us; he came in unto me to lie with me, and I cried with a loud voice: and it came to pass, when he heard that I lifted up my voice and cried, that he left his garment with me, and fled, and got him out. (Genesis 39:12–15)

When Potiphar arrived home, she had her strategy well planned. She lied about Joseph, said that he had tried to seduce her, and then produced his garment that she had grabbed. Potiphar's anger was kindled against Joseph and immediately had him thrown into the prison. It didn't look good for Joseph. He just kept going down. Joseph went down into the pit, and from there into Potiphar's house, a nesting place of evil that would try to destroy him, and from there down into the prison. But God had a plan. He would need a leader during the seven years of famine that He knew was coming, so He sent Joseph to prison.

It doesn't matter where you land or what you must walk through; if you want God to be with you, even as He was with Joseph, you must keep your integrity with God. "But the LORD was with Joseph, and shewed him mercy, and gave him favour in the sight of the keeper of the prison" (Genesis 39:21). Not only was He with Joseph, but He made all that he did to prosper (verse 23).

Joseph's dream took him down before it took him up. The prison experience gave him his final break. If he had not gone down to the prison, he would have never gone up to the king's palace. God had greater things planned for Joseph than just to be a leader over a household. He wanted him to be a leader over a nation. The main thing to remember is that Joseph went down, but he came up. Many times, God allows people to experience failure before arriving at their dream.

It was a beautiful day when Joseph stood before Pharaoh and heard the words that would bring his dream to pass. Pharaoh said:

> Thou shalt be over my house, and according unto thy word shall all my people be ruled: only in the throne will I be greater than thou. And Pharaoh

said unto Joseph, See I have set thee over all the land of Egypt. And Pharaoh took off his ring from his hand, and put it upon Joseph's hand, and arrayed him in vestures of fine linen, and put a gold chain about his neck; and he made him to ride in the second chariot which he had; and they cried before him, Bow the knee: and he made him ruler over all the land of Egypt. (Genesis 41:40–43)

All the people could see were the outward trappings of his leadership: the ring, the fine linen, the chariot, the gold, the pomp, and the glory. They could not see the process: the false accusations, rejection, pain, loneliness, damp prisons, misunderstandings, hatred, fury, blood, a broken heart, and angry lies that marked the pathway to the throne. The glory is always accompanied by suffering and pain. Paul wrote about this concept to Timothy. He said, "If we suffer, we shall also reign with him" (II Timothy 2:12).

SOME PEOPLE HAVE THE MISTAKEN NOTION THAT IF A PERSON IS LIVING RIGHT, EVERYTHING SHOULD GO WELL.

Some people have the mistaken notion that if a person is living right, everything should go well. They look at Psalm 1:3, which describes the blessing of the person who delights in God, "And he shall be like a tree planted by the rivers of water, that bringeth forth his fruit in his season; his leaf also shall not wither; and whatsoever he doeth shall prosper." It is true that whatever he does will prosper, but it is also true that he will be tried in the fire.

Joseph's path was mapped out by God to bring about a great work, and even though he experienced trials, he still prospered wherever he was placed. All the bad situations he was thrust into were because of someone else's scheming. Joseph did not choose his pathway. It was chosen by others. But God allowed it for a higher purpose. He had more planned for Joseph than just to be the favorite son of his father and watch the flock on a hillside.[3]

> He sent a man before them, even Joseph, who was sold for a servant: whose feet they hurt with fetters: he was laid in iron: until the time that his word came: the word of the LORD tried him [to put iron in his soul]. (Psalm 105:17–19)

It was all in God's plan for Joseph's life, to prepare him for future leadership over the whole land. Joseph summed it up in these words, when Joseph's brothers fell before him and repented of what they had done: "Fear not: for am I in the place of God? But as for you, ye thought evil against me; but God meant it unto good, to bring to pass, as it is this day, to save much people alive" (Genesis 50:19–20).

With his newly appointed leadership, Joseph also obtained from Pharaoh a wife. "And unto Joseph were born two sons. . . . And Joseph called the name of the first-born Manasseh: For God, said he, hath made me forget all my toil, and all my father's house. And the name of the second called he Ephraim: For God hath caused me to be fruitful in the land of my affliction" (Genesis 41:50–52).

It took a long time for the fruitfulness to show, but God was preparing Joseph through hardship and struggle to do a mammoth job. It's like the story of the caterpillar. A man found a cocoon of a butterfly. One day a small opening appeared, and he watched the butterfly for several hours as it struggled to force its body through the small hole. To develop into a perfect butterfly, it must force its way through the neck of the cocoon by hours of intense struggle.

> Entomologists explain that this pressure to which the moth is subjected is nature's way of forcing a life-giving substance into its wings. Wanting to lessen the seeming trials and struggles of the moth, an observer said, "I'll lessen the pain and struggle of this helpless creature!" With small scissors he snipped the restraining threads to make the moth's emergence painless and effortless. But the creature never developed his wings. For a brief time before its death, it simply crawled instead of flying on rainbow-colored wings. The struggle helped to develop his wings to be able to fly.
>
> Likewise, in God's kingdom, He uses struggles and difficulties to prepare us for the purpose He has planned for us. Sorrow, suffering, trials, and tribulations are wisely designed to grow us into Christlikeness. The refining and developing processes are oftentimes slow, but through grace, we will emerge triumphant![4]

"Bisogna soffrire per essere grandi" [to be great, it is necessary to suffer]. That was the favorite expression of the great singer Enrico Caruso. After

years of difficulty, Caruso achieved fame, but the man communicated more than beautiful music through his voice. A music critic observed, "His is a voice that loves you, but not only a voice, a sympathetic man." Tribulation does that for a person who accepts life's difficulties in the proper spirit.[5]

MOSES

Moses prayed: "Make us glad according to the days wherein thou hast afflicted us, and the years wherein we have seen evil" (Psalm 90:15).

Moses was stripped of everything that was dear to him. His friends, family, place of honor, and connection with the palace were all things of the past. He was running with fear in every footstep, afraid for his life. He was no longer the son of the princess. He was young and hotheaded and had let his temper get him in trouble.

He had killed an Egyptian who was punishing an Israelite, and now Moses' own people were afraid of him. Word spread of what he had done. "Now when Pharaoh heard this thing, he sought to slay Moses. But Moses fled from the face of Pharaoh, and dwelt in the land of Midian: and he sat down by a well" (Exodus 2:15). God sent Moses to the backside of the desert because He knew what had to be done in the life of Moses before he was ready to be the great leader that he would become.

In time, Moses married one of the seven women who had befriended him at the well. They were the daughters of Jethro, the priest.

> And she bare him a son, and he called his name
> Gershom: for he said, I have been a stranger in
> a strange land. And it came to pass in process
> of time, that the king of Egypt died: and the
> children of Israel sighed by reason of the bond-
> age, and they cried, and their cry came up unto
> God by reason of the bondage. And God heard
> their groaning, and God remembered his cove-
> nant with Abraham, with Isaac, and with Jacob.
> (Exodus 3:22–24)

God heard their cry and looked for a deliverer. One day, God said, "He's ready!" and appeared to Moses in a bush that was on fire but would not burn. Moses received the call, for which God had been preparing him for forty years, on a normal day when Moses was herding his sheep on the backside of the desert. When he came to the mountain of God at Horeb, he saw something very unusual. (See Exodus 3:2–6.)

God wanted to use Moses as His instrument of deliverance for His people. Moses didn't have much confidence in himself and was reluctant to go, but God had an answer for every one of Moses' excuses. Moses was tested in the wilderness so God could use him to accomplish His greater work.

Dwight L. Moody summed it up well: "In the first forty years, in Egypt, Moses learned to be a Somebody. In the second forty years, in the wilderness, Moses learned to be a Nobody. In the third forty years, he learned what God can do with a Somebody who is willing to be a Nobody."[6]

Whether it be a Noah who is to build a ship on dry land, an Abraham who is to offer up his only son, or a Moses who is to despise the treasures of Egypt, or a Joshua who is to besiege Jericho in seven days, using no weapons but the blasts of rams' horns, they all act upon God's command, contrary to the dictates of carnal reason, and the Lord gives them a rich reward as a result of their obedient faith.

–SPURGEON [7]

8
GOD HEARS THE CRY OF THE HUMBLE

Heaven knows we need never be ashamed of our tears, for they are rain upon the blinding dust of earth, overlying our hard hearts.
—CHARLES DICKENS[1]

When you are brought low, you are not alone in your feelings of desolation and desperation. The experience was recorded thousands of years ago in Psalm 102:1–4:

> Hear my prayer, O LORD, and let my cry come unto thee. Hide not thy face from me in the day when I am in trouble; incline thine ear unto me. . . . For my days are consumed like smoke. . . . My heart is smitten, and withered like grass; so that I forget to eat my bread.

Then the psalmist transitioned from his complaints to praise and confidence in his God:

> He will regard the prayer of the destitute, and not despise their prayer. This shall be written for the generation to come: and the people which shall be created shall praise the LORD. (Psalm 102:17–18)

In your times of desperate need, hold on to the Word. Pray it. Talk of it. Speak it. Think it.

> In the beginning was the Word, and the Word was with God, and the Word was God. . . . And the Word was made flesh, and dwelt among us. (John 1:1, 14)

In the beginning, the Word spoke a word, and the lights came on in the heavens. The same creative power works in us. When we read the Word of God, lights come on in our minds. It brings clarity of thought and understanding and gives hope. (See Psalm 119:81, 130, 169.) It also gives us examples of other people who have gone through severe trials.

When Haman sent out letters that all Jews, both young and old, were to be killed, Esther 4:1 records that "Mordecai rent his clothes, put on sackcloth with ashes, and went out into the midst of the city, and cried with a loud and a bitter cry."

This cry was heard by Queen Esther and resulted in her telling Mordecai to have the Jews fast and pray for three days. She said, "I also and my maidens will fast likewise; and so will I go unto the king, which is not according to the law: and if I perish, I perish" (Esther 4:16).

God heard their cry, and instead of their death, Haman was put to death on the very gallows he had planned to use to kill Mordecai. Instead of death, "The Jews had light, and gladness, and joy, and honour" (Esther 8:16).

One of the most desperate cries in the Scriptures is a song written by Heman in Psalm 88:1-4, 6:

> O LORD God of my salvation, I have cried day and night before thee: let my prayer come before thee: incline thine ear unto my cry; for my soul is full of troubles: and my life draweth nigh unto the grave. I am counted with them that go down into the pit: I am as a man that hath no strength. . . . Thou hast laid me in the lowest pit, in darkness, in the deeps.

His prayer affirmed his faith by continuing to ask God for help: "But unto thee have I cried, O LORD" (Psalm 88:13).

THE CRY

In Exodus 2 the children of Israel, who were slaves in Egypt at the time, suffered under harsh conditions and cruel taskmasters. "They cried, and their cry came up unto God by reason of the bondage. And God heard their groaning, and God remembered his covenant with Abraham, with Isaac, and with Jacob" (Exodus 2:23-24). The Lord said He had seen the affliction of His people and "heard their cry by reason of their taskmasters; for I know their sorrows" (Exodus 3:7).

Listen to what God said:

- I've seen the afflictions of my people.
- I've heard their cry.
- I know their sorrow.

God in Heaven heard the cry of His people on earth. His ears are open to our cries. David talked about this in his song of deliverance in Psalm 18:6 after the slaying of the four sons of the giant: "In my distress I called upon the LORD, and cried unto my God: he heard my voice out of his temple, and my cry came before him, even into his ears." (See also II Samuel 22:7.) Verses 8–16 of the same chapter describe how God responded to David's cry, and verse 17 is the end result: "He delivered me from my strong enemy, and from them which hated me: for they were too strong for me."

When you're in a situation that is bigger than you can handle and those working against you seem to be stronger than you are, remember God is on your side. With God you have nothing to fear. "What shall we then say to these things? If God be for us, who can be against us?" (Romans 8:31).

When God hears the cry of the desperate, His heart is moved with compassion, and He comes down and works in a miraculous way. It's always victory with Him.

In Solomon's prayer for the dedication of the Temple in I Kings 8:26, he prayed, "O God of Israel, let thy word, I pray thee, be verified, which thou spakest unto thy servant David my father." Solomon was saying, "Confirm Thy

Word. Prove Thy Word! Let Thy Word be demonstrated." When God gives you a word from His Word, you can say, "Let Thy Word be verified!" God is obligated to His Word, but it operates according to His schedule.

Solomon's prayer continues in verse 29: "That thine eyes may be open toward this house night and day, even toward the place of which thou hast said, My name shall be there: that thou mayest hearken unto the prayer which thy servant shall make."

> SOMETIMES YOU CRY, AND IT FEELS LIKE HE ISN'T LISTENING.

The name of the Lord is our refuge. Proverbs 18:10 says, "The name of the LORD is a strong tower: the righteous runneth into it, and is safe." The opening of Psalm 61 also demonstrates this:

> Hear my cry, O God; attend unto my prayer. From the end of the earth will I cry unto thee, when my heart is overwhelmed: lead me to the rock that is higher than I. For thou hast been a shelter for me, and a strong tower from the enemy. (Psalm 61:1–3)

Sometimes you cry, and it feels like He isn't listening. David wrote about feeling this way: "My God, my God, why hast thou forsaken me? why art thou so far from helping me, and from the words of my roaring? O my God, I cry in the daytime, but thou hearest not; and in the night season, and am not silent" (Psalm 22:1–2).

Jesus, who was God manifested in the flesh, echoed this psalm of David when He cried out on the cross, "My God, why hast thou forsaken me?" He wasn't forsaken, but He felt like He was. The eternal plan of God was at work. A great victory that would smash Satan's head was soon to take place. God was watching all the time. (Just like He watches us all the time.)

Matthew 6 says the birds are taken care of by the Father. Verse 26 asks, "Are ye not much better than they?" He takes care of the lilies of the field, and how much more will He take care of you? He sees every sparrow that falls to the ground, and you are in that "how much more" category when it comes to God's care for you.

It is hard to wait. The time of silence compares to the story told of seamen in the doldrums:

> Nothing was so feared by seamen in the days when ocean vessels were driven by wind and sail, as the doldrums. The doldrums is a part of the ocean near the equator, abounding in calms, squalls, and light, baffling winds. There the weather is hot and extremely dispiriting. The old sailing vessels, when caught in the doldrums, would lie helpless for days and weeks, waiting for the wind to begin to blow.[2]

Even when it feels like God is not listening, He heard you before you called and knew your needs before you needed them.

GOD HEARS

In Psalm 39, David prayed, "Remove thy stroke away from me: I am consumed by the blow of thine hand. . . . Hear my prayer, O LORD, and give ear unto my cry; hold not thy peace at my tears: for I am a stranger with thee. . . . O spare me, that I may recover strength, before I go hence, and be no more" (Psalm 39:10, 12, 13). David was at the end.

But in the next chapter he wrote, "I waited patiently for the LORD; and he inclined unto me, and heard my cry. He brought me up also out of an horrible pit, out of the miry clay, and set my feet upon a rock, and established my goings. And he hath put a new song in my mouth. . . . Blessed is that man that maketh the LORD his trust" (Psalm 40:1–4).

Three of the most important things you can lean on during a time of desperation are the Word of God, the name of the Lord, and prayer to God.

During this time pray, pray, and pray some more. Pray in the morning, pray in the daytime, pray day and night, and God will avenge you, according to Luke 18.

Prayer is powerful! It clears the vision, steadies the nerves, defines duty, and stiffens the purpose. Prayer gives power, fire, and enthusiasm. It is flesh touching glory. It can change any situation and bring lasting results. Prayer is our connection with God.

Without prayer we are as fish out of water, gasping for air. Prayer is your connection to the power line. Prayer does for your soul what breathing does for your body.

Scientists have proven that when a person prays, negative thoughts are changed to positive ones. Dark, negative, and even suicidal thoughts decline as a person prays, and if one prays often enough, those thoughts will be dominated by a sense of power and well-being.

Prayer brings peace. No matter what obstacle, disappointment, or stress you are experiencing, God has come to give you peace. You can face this storm with confidence because He is the master of the storm. Speak these words when you feel fear or are overwhelmed: "These things I have spoken unto you, that in me ye might have peace. In the world ye shall have tribulation: but be of good cheer; I have overcome the world" (John 16:33). I know it works, because it happened to me on June 11, 2016, and is dated in my Bible.

When you pray, you get a glimpse of eternity, and your world becomes larger. Prayer helps to organize the mind. It energizes you. Prayer is a place of refuge where one meets with God. Without prayer, a person becomes a dry, thirsty land and opens himself to depression. Chrysostom said, "The man without prayer is as a city without walls and open to all attacks." Prayer is a spiritual covering for the mind and heart. Protection and healing are in God's presence.

YOUR SPIRITUAL BATTERY RUNS DOWN WITHOUT PRAYER.

Your spiritual battery runs down without prayer. It's important to plug in to the power source. Across the world at nighttime people plug in their iPhones and iPads. The devices are dead, depleted, or low on power. It's imperative that we plug in daily to our divine source of power. Prayer is frail humanity connecting to divinity, and the

God who has all power will send a spiritual charge into your soul and spirit.

David said in Psalm 55:16–17: "As for me, I will call upon God; and the LORD shall save me. Evening, and morning, and at noon, will I pray, and cry aloud: and he shall hear my voice."

What you want tomorrow, you must pray today. You live tomorrow in today's prayers. "Ask, and it shall be given you: seek, and ye shall find; knock, and it shall be opened unto you" (Matthew 7:7).

- Daniel prayed, and God delivered him from the lions' den the next day.
- Hannah prayed and received her miracle nine months later.
- Peter was put in prison to be kept until after Easter, "But prayer was made without ceasing of the church unto God for him" (Acts 12:5). His answer came in the nighttime while they were praying. God sent an angel and delivered Peter! Herod was shocked and displeased at this great miracle wrought by prayer.
- Elisha said to the prophet Elijah, "I pray thee, let a double portion of thy spirit be upon me." Elijah answered, "Thou hast asked a hard thing: nevertheless, if thou see me when I am taken from thee, it shall be so unto thee; but if not, it shall not be so" (II Kings 2:9–10).

Elisha made sure he saw Elijah being taken up. When Elijah was caught up in a chariot of fire in a whirlwind, Elisha saw it and cried,

My father, my father, the chariot of Israel, and the horsemen thereof. And he saw him no more: and he took hold of his own clothes, and rent them in two pieces. He took up also the mantle of Elijah that fell from him, and went back, and stood by the bank of Jordan; and he took the mantle of Elijah that fell from him, and smote the waters, and said, Where is the LORD God of Elijah? and when he also had smitten the waters, they parted hither and thither: and Elisha went over. (II Kings 2:12–14)

Elisha had his first miracle; he had thirteen to go before he had doubled Elijah's seven miracles. The prayer and prophecy were not fulfilled until after his death. The fourteenth miracle came when a dead soldier was hastily thrown on the bones of Elisha. The young man came alive, making it miracle number fourteen. (See II Kings 13:20–21).

The Lord, when He hath given great faith, has been known to try it by long delayings. But we must be careful not to take delays in prayers for denials. God keeps a file for our prayers—they are not blown away by the wind, they are treasured in the King's archives. There is a registry in the court of heaven wherein every prayer is recorded. Tried believer, the Lord hath a tear-bottle in which the costly drops of sacred grief are put away, and a book in which thy holy groanings are numbered.[3]

Prayer is the most important thing you can do. If they stacked free gold in the prayer room how many people would be there to receive it? Prayers of saints are more precious to God than fine gold and are stored in golden vials (Revelation 5:8).

When you're desperate you don't care what others think about you.

- Eli accused Hannah of being drunk in the temple, but she didn't care — she needed a miracle.
- Blind Bartimaeus cried even louder.
- The widow woman came to the judge every day asking to be avenged, and the judge said, "Yet because this widow troubleth me, I will avenge her, lest by her continual coming she weary me" (Luke 18:5).

God is faithful to His Word.

The eyes of the LORD are upon the righteous, and his ears are open unto their cry. . . . The righteous cry, and the LORD heareth, and delivereth them out of all their troubles. (Psalm 34:15, 17)

He giveth to the beast his food, and to the young ravens which cry. (Psalm 147:9)

When he maketh inquisition for blood, he remembereth them: he forgetteth not the cry of the humble. (Psalm 9:12)

So that they cause the cry of the poor to come unto him, and he heareth the cry of the afflicted. (Job 34:28)

These six things doth the LORD hate: yea, seven are an abomination unto him: A proud look, a lying tongue, and hands that shed innocent blood. (Proverbs 6:16–17)

God opposes the proud but shows favor to the humble. (James 4:6, NIV)

Humble yourselves in the sight of the Lord, and he shall lift you up. (James 4:10)

If my people, which are called by my name, shall humble themselves, and pray, and seek my face, and turn from their wicked ways; then will I hear from heaven, and will forgive their sin, and will heal their land. (II Chronicles 7:14)

God listens to the humble in heart but resists the proud. He fills the humble with His Spirit and sits on the throne of their heart.

Just as water seeks to fill the lowest places, so
God fills you with His glory and power, when
He finds you empty and abased.
–ANDREW MURRAY[4]

Outward losses drive good people to their
prayers, but bad people to their curses.
–MATTHEW HENRY[5]

9
BROKEN THINGS

No pain, no balm: no thorns, no throne; no gall,
no glory; no cross, no crown.
–William Penn[1]

> The saddest day has a morrow
> The darkest night had a dawn
> So turn from yesterday's sorrow
> And press courageously on![2]

In April 2018, God brought the following memory to my mind and impressed me to share it in this chapter.

In 1974, after my mother had suffered with cancer, I invited her, Daddy, and my little sister to live with us so I could take care of her. I just knew I was going to nurse her back to health and that God was going to heal her! T. W. Barnes, the faith healer, prayed for her over the phone, we gave her the healthiest food and the best care, but the Lord chose to take her seven months later, on December 18, 1974. It was one of the saddest days of my life when I had to say goodbye to my wonderful mother. My health was affected because of the heavy loads leading to this moment. We had four children at the time, and the care of my family, including my sister and mother and father, the responsibilities of a pastor's wife, and the position of my house as the meeting place for all the family to visit Mother took their toll. About a month after Mother passed, I started having health problems. My chest felt heavy, there was pain, and I had trouble breathing. My sweet husband took me to the family doctor, Dr. Sanders, where they did an EKG and examined me. The tests came back negative, showing no evidence of a heart problem. It was a good report, but the symptoms didn't go away. My husband kept taking me to Dr. Sanders every time I'd have an attack. Finally, one day before he did another EKG, he asked me, "Have you had anything traumatic happen in your life recently?" I told him about my mother and started crying. He said, "The symptoms you are having are from a broken heart! They can feel the same as a heart attack."

I'll never forget what happened that day! My husband drove me home and then went back to the church, and I went into the house and walked down the hallway and glanced into the bedroom where Mother and Dad had stayed while they lived with us. The house was empty; the children were in school. I felt sad, heavy-hearted, broken, and weary, so I went in our bedroom and laid on the bed. Then it happened.

The minute my head hit the pillow, I felt my spirit leave my body and travel upward. It went up, up, up until I came to a golden meadow with golden tables. All the people were happy and radiant and talked to one another. Then I saw my mother. She was so happy! Her hair was dark brown (when she died it was gray), and as I saw her, she turned and saw me. We started walking toward one another. When I reached out to touch her, I felt my spirit go back to my body. It was so vivid I remember every detail. From that day forward I started to heal, and I immersed myself in the Bible, studying it ferociously. <u>God set my soul on fire with His Word</u> and inspired me to start Radiant Life classes. The first ones began in September 1975, and we continued teaching the ladies for twenty-five years. The material God quickened to my heart was rich, and the ladies were loving it, learning how to be radiant women. When our youngest child was born, my husband said to me, "You're going to be home now with the baby. This would be a good time for you to consider putting all this material in book form." Little did he know where the publishing of the first book in 1980 would lead. It's been reprinted eight times, and this book will be the sixty-second book God has put in my heart to write.

It all started with my broken heart and broken dreams. God truly uses broken things for His glory! Life took on new meaning, and the needs of people became more apparent when I became aware of their needs, as illustrated in the poem below:

CHAPTER 9

GOD, LET ME BE AWARE

God, let me be aware.
Let me not stumble blindly down life's ways,
Just seeking somehow safely to get through the days,
Hand never groping for another hand,
Not even wondering why it all was planned,
Eyes to the ground, unseeking for the light,
Soul never longing for a wild wing flight,
Please, keep me eager just to do my share.
God, let me be aware.

God, let me be aware,
Stab my soul fiercely with others' pain,
Let me walk seeing horror and stain.
Let my hand, groping, find other hands.
Give me the heart that divines, understands.
Give me the courage, wounded, to fight,
Fill me with knowledge and drench me with light.
Please, keep me eager just to do my share.
God, let me be aware.
    –MIRIAM TEICHNER[3]

People often overlook it, but Jesus said the second commandment is to love our neighbor as ourselves (Mark 12:31). Coldness toward others in their plight is an offense to God. As we treat others, it will come back to us.

In 2013, two years after the Lord had promoted my husband, Kenneth Haney, to Heaven, I was going through some of his messages and found one entitled "Life in Reality." It was about broken things. When God first quickened the thought of this book to me in 2014, it seemed rather negative, so I just typed the title into the computer along with the verse of Scripture He showed me and left it there. He would give me little tidbits here and there, and I'd add them to the file. He gave me some of the reasons for having been brought low, and then I remembered the following message that my husband had preached and knew God wanted it to be inserted here.

In 2016, He kept coming to me more forcefully, and I thought it was time to obey His voice and complete what He wanted me to write. But He had other plans. On April 5, 2018, Missionary Louie Louw told me, "It could be that God was preparing you for what was going to happen on May 6, 2016. It was preparatory for the finishing of the book." That stayed with me, and the more I thought on it, I agreed. So finally, here are portions of the message Bishop Haney preached:

"Broken Things"

Jeremiah 4:3: "For thus saith the LORD to the men of Judah and Jerusalem, Break up your fallow ground, and sow not among thorns."

Through the Refiner's fire, we are purified.

1. As when Joseph was sold, betrayed, and placed in prison.
2. When God stirs the nest as mentioned in Deuteronomy 32:11.

Again, the Bible tells us all about these things. Deuteronomy 32:11 (NIV) says, "Like an eagle that stirs up its nest [makes it uncomfortable] and hovers over its young [showing them how to fly], that spreads its wings to catch them [as He pushes them out of the nest] and carries them aloft," so is the Lord God to His people.

God is out to mature us. Because we were made to fly, He will stir up our nest—our world. We weren't made to languish in the comfortable surroundings of our nest-like world. We're created in the image of God, made to fly and train our young to do the same. You and I were made to soar, but sometimes we simply don't know it or forget it, so there are times when God will push us out of the nest.

The *Jamieson-Fausset-Brown Bible Commentary* explains how Deuteronomy 32:11 relates to God.

This beautiful and expressive metaphor is founded on the extraordinary care and attachment with which the female eagle cherishes her young. . . . She, in their first attempts at flying, supports them on the tip of her wing, encouraging, directing, and aiding their feeble efforts to longer and sublimer flights. So did God take the most tender and powerful care of His chosen people.

Then suddenly one day, when the eaglets have grown to flying age, the eagle with its powerful talons, begins digging, taking out the feathers, the leaves and dislodging all that made life comfortable. They start to feel the prick of the thorns on the branches that now have dried and become brittle, and no longer is the nest soft and comfortable, and they squirm and wonder what's going on. Then the mother eagle rises straight above, and furiously beats its wings, stirring everything until the eaglet jumps up on the edge of the nest.

"God, like the eagle, stirs our nest. Yesterday it was the place for us; today there is a new plan. He wrecks the nest, although He knows it is dear to us; perhaps because it is dear to us. He loves us too well not to spoil our meager contentment" (Mrs. Charles Cowman).

Broken things are more valuable: A bar of steel is worth $25, horseshoes $75, but delicate watch springs many thousands. The farmer does not spend time tilling the sand hill that has no value to crops but spends most of his time preparing soil with promise of the future.

Job said: "He knoweth the way that I take: when he hath tried me, I shall come forth as gold." Break up your fallow ground; this was the message of Jeremiah.

1. Dark days were setting in upon the nation of Israel
2. Trusting in her false security permitted the enemy to rule her nation and the peoples' lives.
3. The people of Israel had longed for ease and comfort.
4. The Lord compared the nation to fallow ground. Fallow ground is permitted to lie idle and uncultivated, providing no grain or fruit but weeds and thorns, as described in Matthew 13, the Parable of Soils: wayside, stony, thorny, and good ground.

Before a thing can be made, there must be a breaking!

1. Before a house is built, a tree must be broken down.
2. Before the foundation can be laid, the rock must be blasted from the quarry bed.
3. Before the ripe grain can cover the field, the ground must be broken.
4. John 12:24: "Except a corn of wheat fall into the ground and die, it abideth alone; but if it die, it bringeth forth much fruit."

LIFE IN REALITY

Broken dreams, broken promises, and broken hopes: *We cast the broken things aside and call them junk, but God casts the unbroken things aside as useless!*

After Joshua's death, Israel was vexed by the repeated attacks of her enemies. Israel cried out for deliverance, and God raised up a man named Gideon. Gideon and his men were facing a Midianite army to the north. Then the Lord said to Gideon, "The people that are with thee are too many for me to give the Midianites into their hands, lest Israel vaunt themselves against me, saying, Mine own hand hath saved me. Now therefore go to, proclaim in the ears of the people, saying, Whosoever is fearful and afraid, let him return and depart early from mount Gilead. And there returned of the people twenty and two thousand; and there remained ten thousand." Then the Lord said to him, "The people are yet too many; bring them down unto the water, and I will try them for thee there: and it shall be, that of whom I say unto thee, This shall go with thee, the same shall go with thee; and of whomsoever I say unto thee. This shall not go with thee, the same shall not go." (See Judges 7:2–4).

Thus, Gideon followed the instructions of the Lord concerning his God-ordained assignment:

1. The first thing he did was tell all the fearful and afraid to depart and go home.
2. The second thing he did was to reduce the army further as God had instructed. When they went to the brook, God said to take with him all those who lapped like a dog, and all who bowed on their knees were released to go home. So now Gideon was down to three hundred men.

3. Gideon gave each man a trumpet, an empty pitcher, and a lamp to place inside the pitcher. Then he divided the three men into three companies. "And the three companies blew the trumpets, and brake the pitchers, and held the lamps in their left hands, and the trumpets in their right hands to blow withal: and they cried, The sword of the LORD, and of Gideon" (Judges 7:20).

God used a broken pitcher that revealed the light inside—a type of the Holy Ghost fire, a blazing torch that would someday be in earthen vessels. "But we have this treasure in earthen vessels, that the excellency of the power may be of God, and not of us" (II Corinthians 4:7).

Gideon had no victory until pitchers were broken. Trials, hardships, and troubles break us but also prepare us for God's intervention. Before God's power can be shown, there is always a crisis.

There would have been no redemption for the sins of the world without the broken body of Christ at Calvary. First Corinthians 11:24 says "And when he had given thanks, he brake it, and said, Take, eat: this is my body, which is broken for you: this do in remembrance of me."

God makes only what He breaks and breaks only what He wants to use.

1. Three times Peter denied Jesus, and when Jesus looked at him, he wept bitterly. He became the spokesman on the Day of Pentecost and was greatly used of God.

2. On the day of Isaiah's greatest loss, he cried, "In the year that king Uzziah died, I saw also the Lord sitting upon a throne, high and lifted up, and his train filled the temple" (Isaiah 6:1). Then he cried, "Woe is me! . . . because I am a man of unclean lips" (Isaiah 6:5).
3. Jeremiah said, The potter started over and "made it again." (See Jeremiah 18:1-6.)
4. Jacob was a different man by the time he returned to Bethel.
5. Before Jesus could feed the five thousand, He had to break the bread.
6. Before the four friends could get the sick man to Jesus, they had to break the roof open.

He must increase, but I must decrease. (John 3:30)

And he said unto me, My grace is sufficient for thee: for my strength is made perfect in weakness. (II Corinthians 12:9)

God will have no strength used in His battles but the strength in which He imparts. Are you mourning over your weakness? Take courage, for there must be a consciousness of weakness before the Lord will give thee victory. -SPURGEON[4]

10
HE HAS BROUGHT ME LOW SO I CAN SOAR

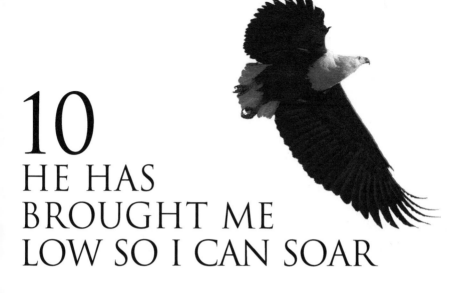

Deep, unspeakable suffering may well be called a baptism, a regeneration, the initiation into a new state.
–George Eliot[1]

[Good men] should not shrink from hardships and difficulties, nor complain against fate; they should take in good part whatever happens, and should turn it to good. Not what you endure, but how you endure, is important.
–SENECA THE YOUNGER[2]

A rancher rounding up cattle in the high, rugged terrain of the mountains discovered an eagle's nest. Carefully picking up one of the eggs, he brought it back to the ranch, went to the chicken yard, and placed it under a setting hen.

In the process of time, the eggs hatched. Along with the little chicks, an eaglet pecked his way through the shell. It was a strange sight to see the mother hen leading her tiny chicks, scratching for worms along with the odd-looking eaglet attempting to act like one of hers. As the days passed it became quite evident that there was a distinct difference between the eaglet and the small chickens. Yet for some reason he became the product of his environment, scratching for worms, wading in the chicken pen, and roosting a few feet off the ground on the perch provided by man. They were all dependent on the rancher to bring them food each day. Every so often the little eagle would stretch and look straight into the sky. It appeared that something within him, an instinct, a call of the wild, a purpose for his creation was calling him beyond the pen. Yet because of his unusual environment he was subject to being dependent upon man.

One day after he had reached full growth, a soaring eagle cried from high above. That cry was a call to his very nature. He was not born to live in a pen, subject to being fed by man, scratching for worms along with chickens. His call and created purpose was to soar in the sun, to live in the rugged terrain and the heights of nature. Soon the eagle was flapping his wings, and with great effort he began to fly. He flew out of the pen and began to soar as his wings grew stronger and stronger. He flew away to live in his own realm.

The eagle, for some time, had become the product of his environment. He scratched with the chickens, ate from the hands of man, roosted a few feet off the ground, and lived within the confines of a chicken coop. Those around him lived that way, yet his instinct and nature called him to soar to the mountaintops. We, too, who were born in the family of God—God's children—were called to live in a realm not of this world.

Sometimes on your journey God leads you down a road that takes you to unfamiliar territory, and it can cause you to be fearful. That's the time to remember the greatness of your God, His promise to take care of you, and the assurance that nothing can touch you that He does not allow. You are in safe hands.

When it looks like it's over, that's just the beginning for a miracle in your life. The story told in Exodus 14 of Moses crossing the Red Sea is not just a Sunday school story. This is about the magnitude of our God. We're talking about two to three million people on foot, fleeing for their lives from Egypt, where they had served as slaves, beaten and under bondage. Suddenly they looked

> WHEN IT LOOKS LIKE IT'S OVER, THAT'S JUST THE BEGINNING FOR A MIRACLE IN YOUR LIFE.

back and could see in the distance the Egyptian army pursuing them. Josephus commented that this consisted of six hundred choice chariots, fifty thousand horsemen, and two hundred thousand footmen, all armed. Another historian speculated there were twenty thousand chariots destroyed that day.

Panic-stricken the Israelites cried, "Why have you brought us out here in the wilderness to die?" Moses spoke faith before it was done. "Fear ye not, stand still, and see the salvation of the LORD, which he shall shew to you to day: for the Egyptians whom ye have seen to day, ye shall see them again no more for ever. The LORD shall fight for you" (Exodus 14:13–14).

God caused a strong east wind to blow that dried the pathway that had opened when Moses stretched his hand over the Red Sea. The pathway is said to have been between one to two miles wide, and several million Israelites crossed it in one night. While they were crossing, the Lord hid them with a cloud. It was a huge cloud to cover several million people, but as soon as they were out of danger, God removed the cloud and let the enemy see them. That's when Pharaoh gave the order to pursue. As soon as all the army, men, horses, and chariots were well within the middle of the Red Sea, God told Moses to stretch forth his hand. The waters that stood in heaps on both sides were released into a roaring flood of death which covered all the Egyptian hosts. Not one escaped. And their dead bodies floated to the seashore. Although it looked like the end for the Israelites, God set an ambush for Pharaoh and his army. God was going to be glorified through this impossible situation.

The enemy was behind them, chasing them and causing them fear and distress. It looked like there were more with the enemy than there were with the Israelites. The enemy had horses and chariots. The Hebrews had none, but they had God.

> Some trust in chariots, and some in horses: but we will remember the name of the LORD our God. They are brought down and fallen: but we are risen, and stand upright. (Psalm 20:7–8)

Therefore I will look unto the LORD: I will wait for
the God of my salvation: my God will hear me.
Rejoice not against me, O mine enemy; when I
fall, I shall arise; when I sit in darkness, the LORD
shall be a light unto me. (Micah 7:7–8)

Rule 1 — The Lord shall fight for you.
Moses recorded the law of warfare in
Deuteronomy 20:1–4:

When thou goest out to battle against thine enemies, and seest horses, and chariots, and a people
more than thou, be not afraid of them: for the
LORD thy God is with thee, which brought thee up
out of the land of Egypt. And it shall be, when ye
are come nigh unto the battle, that the priest shall
approach and speak unto the people, and shall
say unto them, Hear, O Israel, ye approach this
day unto battle against your enemies: let not your
hearts faint, fear not, and do not tremble, neither
be ye terrified because of them; for the LORD your
God is he that goeth with you, to fight for you
against your enemies, to save you.

Rule 2 — Fear not; the Lord is with you.
Joshua learned this from Moses. Some of Joshua's last
words to Israel are recorded in Joshua 23:3, 10:

Ye have seen all that the LORD your God hath
done unto all these nations because of you; for the
LORD your God is he that hath fought for you. . . .

One man of you shall chase a thousand: for the LORD your God, he it is that fighteth for you, as he hath promised you.

Joshua was remembering the battle and victory at Gibeon. On the day he fought against the five Amorite kings and their armies, the Lord told him: "Fear them not: for I have delivered them into thine hand" (Joshua 10:8). The Bible says the Lord discomfited them and slew them with a great slaughter at Gibeon. As they fled, the Lord cast great stones from heaven upon them, and they died. Time was running out; there were more armies to fight. That's when Joshua spoke to the Lord and said,

Sun, stand thou still upon Gibeon; and thou, Moon, in the valley of Ajalon. And the sun stood still, and the moon stayed, until the people had avenged themselves upon their enemies. . . . So the sun . . . hasted not to go down about a whole day. And there was no day like that before it or after it, that the LORD hearkened unto the voice of a man: for the LORD fought for Israel. (Joshua 10:12–14)

Rule 3—The Lord will empower you.

It happened to Jehoshaphat. Judah was surrounded and afraid, so they prayed, fasted, and told God, "We don't know what to do, but our eyes are upon You! We will die without Your help."

God sent this answer to their prayer and fasting: "Ye shall not need to fight in this battle; . . . fear not, nor be dismayed; to morrow go out against them: for the LORD will be with you" (II Chronicles 20:17).

They went out singing, "Praise the LORD; for His mercy endureth for ever." While they went out unafraid, singing unto the Lord, the Lord Himself sent ambushments and slew all the enemy who had come up against them.

No matter where you are at in life, no matter what you're going through, just remember that with God on your side you are a majority! With God all things are possible. God is working in your life. His plan is bigger than our finite minds can grasp, but He makes no mistakes.

God remembers every prayer you have prayed. He never forgets. If He chooses to lead you down an unexpected pathway and maybe not do things the way you expected, just

> GOD REMEMBERS EVERY PRAYER YOU HAVE PRAYED. HE NEVER FORGETS.

trust in Him, for He will walk with you and take you places you've never been.

To have God with you and to fight for you is an awesome privilege. Bill Thompson, a missionary to Colombia for over thirty years, once spent the night in a small, primitive farmhouse in the mountains above a village. He was awakened the next morning by a man inspecting the outside of the house.

"Where are the connections for the lights?" the man asked.

"What lights do you mean?" Thompson responded. "There are none here."

"Last night, some hired killers were sent from the village to harm you," the man said. "But they saw guards on the roof with bright spotlights, so they did not come near. Where are the wires that powered the lights?" Then Bill Thompson began to tell him about God and His guardian angels.

But God doesn't always send angels. Sometimes God uses pressure to work something great in your life.

When trials in life seem to be too much for you, remember the apostle Paul felt this way also. He actually wanted to die. The greater the pressure upon us, the greater is our realization of our helplessness, with the result that our dependence upon God is greater and we receive spiritual power.

> For we would not, brethren, have you ignorant of our trouble which came to us in Asia, that we were pressed out of measure, above strength, insomuch that we despaired even of life. (II Corinthians 1:8)

> Pressed out of measure and pressed out of length
> Pressed so intensely it seems without strength
> Pressed in the body and pressed in the soul
> Pressed in the mind til the dark surges roll
> Pressure by foes, and pressure by friends,
> Pressure on pressure til life nearly ends;
> Pressed into loving the staff and the rod,
> Pressed into knowing no help but God;
> Pressed into liberty where nothing clings,

Pressed into faith for impossible things;
Pressed into living a life in the Lord,
Pressed into living a Christ-life outpoured.[3]

Paul wasn't the only person in the Bible who experienced pressure and thought about giving up. The destitute widow and her son were going to eat their last meal and die. It was the last bit of food in the house. They had no money and no one to help them. She was just a lonely, poor widow with one son. They were at the end of their rope. She thought it was time to die, but God had other plans. We find the story in I Kings 17:8–16. God looked down and decided to turn her hopelessness to hope. He spoke to Elijah and told him to go to Zarephath, for a certain woman there was going to feed him.

When Elijah arrived at her house, she was picking up sticks to build a fire. He asked her to bring him a drink of water. As she went to get it, he hollered to her and said, "Bring me some bread to go with it." That is when her hopelessness revealed itself. "And she said, As the LORD thy God liveth, I have not a cake, but an handful of meal in a barrel, and a little oil in a cruse: and, behold, I am gathering two sticks, that I may go in and dress it for me and my son, that we may eat it, and die" (I Kings 17:12).

Death was in her mind. You cannot get much lower than that. She was hopeless, and stretched to the limit without anywhere to turn when Elijah uttered those immortal words, "Fear not!"

She thought, *All my food is gone, my money is gone, and my husband is dead. I am all alone. There is absolutely nothing left to live for. We are getting ready to die.* She was consumed with fear. She was afraid of the future and afraid of the present—the awful burden of providing for her son but not knowing how to do it. Into that hopeless despair thundered the words, "Fear not!"

Elijah did not say, "Praise the Lord!" He did not berate her and say, "You're a foolish woman to want to die and give up. What's wrong with you anyhow?" He simply went to the root of the problem and said, "Fear not!"

After he told her not to fear, he asked her to do something impossible. She had just told him that she had only enough meal and oil to make one more cake. Elijah told her to make him one first and to bring it to him. Then he told her to make another for herself and her son, but Elijah did not make these commands without a promise. He promised her if she would take this step of faith, God would take care of her. "For thus saith the LORD God of Israel, The barrel of meal shall not waste, neither shall the cruse of oil fail, until the day that the LORD sendeth rain upon the earth" (I Kings 17:14).

She listened and believed. Her actions proved this. "And she went and did according to the saying of Elijah: and she, and he, and her house, did eat many days" (I Kings 17:15).

Because of her obedience and faith, God worked a miracle, "And the barrel of meal wasted not, neither did the cruse of oil fail, according to the word of the LORD, which he spake by Elijah" (I Kings 17:16). The source of the trial became the source of her blessing.

Man's extremity is God's opportunity. Extremities are a warrant for opportunities. A man at his wit's end is not at his faith's end." –Matthew Henry

During your moment of fear, whether it's fear of death, fear of people, fear of an outcome, or any other kind of fear, find a place to pray. Pray the Word, for it has power. When anxiety comes upon you, go immediately to God and get into His presence. His presence will bring peace. You cannot always control what happens in your life, but you can control your response. Do what Elijah told the widow to do, "Fear not!" Then obey God's Word.

> Trust in the LORD with all thine heart; and lean not unto thine own understanding. In all thy ways acknowledge him, and he shall direct thy paths. (Proverbs 3:5-6)

This is what the widow of Zarephath did. She could not control her situation, but she controlled her response to Elijah. She obeyed what he spoke to her. She was tense and fearful when relating her situation to him, but after his command of faith, she relaxed and began doing what she could do with what she had. After this, God visited her with a divine miracle.

We are promised His help when we need it, according to Isaiah 40:29-31:

> He giveth power to the faint; and to them that have no might he increaseth strength. Even the youths shall faint and be weary, and the young

men shall utterly fall: but they that wait upon the LORD shall renew their strength; they shall mount up with wings as eagles; they shall run, and not be weary; and they shall walk, and not faint.

The eagle does not escape the storm. It simply uses the storm to lift it higher. It rises on the winds that bring the storm. *When the storms of life come upon us, we can rise above them like the eagle and ride the winds of any storm that brings disappointment, sickness, crisis, and other troublesome things into our lives.*

Many people have been captive to their disappointments and losses until their resignation makes them feel imprisoned. They *think* they are not able to soar and fly. It has become a way of life.

There was a man out west who caught an eagle and kept it in confinement for seventeen years. At last having to move a distance he advertised to sell all his goods at auction, and that at the close of the sale he would liberate the eagle. People came for hundreds of miles to see the bird set free. The auction was over. Low clouds hung over the earth, dark and drear. The cage was opened but the eagle did not move. His master called him, but he stayed inside.

At last his master pulled him out and with all his strength tried to push the bird toward the zenith. His great wings only spread to allow him to settle back to the man's shoulder. The man was nonplussed. Just then there shot through the clouds a bright beam of sunshine straight to the eagle's eye. And the eagle rose as if by magnet towards the source.[4]

Don't allow life to be a thief and rob you of your promise given by Jesus Himself in John 10:10: "The thief cometh not, but for to steal, and to kill, and to destroy: I am come that they might have life, and that they might have it more abundantly."

You can fly and soar again. It may look hopeless, but there's always hope with God. You weren't meant to live shut in a cage; you were meant to soar and have abundant life. It's time to rally the forces and fight

> YOU CAN FLY AND
> SOAR AGAIN.

back for what is rightfully yours as a child of God.

Satan desperately wishes to control the mind. He wants to keep you in a chicken pen instead of letting you soar like you were born to do. His way of controlling humanity is through the mind; likewise, Christ's way of fulfilling His purpose on earth through His anointed ones is by possessing their minds. The apostle Paul said,

> For though we walk in the flesh, we do not war after the flesh; (for the weapons of our warfare are not carnal, but mighty through God to the pulling down of strong holds;) casting down imaginations, and every high thing that exalteth itself against the knowledge of God, and bringing

into captivity every thought to the obedience of Christ. (II Corinthians 10:3–5)

You may feel like all is lost, but you need to get up and fight like Sir Winston Churchill rallied to inspire a nation.

Days after Dunkirk were dark days. All seemed lost. England lay prostrate. Forty-seven warships had been sunk in the operations off Norway after Dunkirk. When the evacuation was completed, half the British destroyers were in the shipyards for repairs while the Royal Air Force had lost forty percent of its bomber strength. Britain was on the brink of famine and her armies were without arms or equipment. They had left in France 50,000 vehicles.

Churchill spoke with fire in his voice for the defenseless islanders and put new fight in them:

"We shall not flag nor fail. We shall go on to the end. We shall fight in France and on the seas and oceans; we shall fight with growing confidence and growing strength in the air. We shall defend our island whatever the cost may be; we shall fight on beaches, landing grounds, in fields, in streets and on the hills. We shall never surrender and even if, which I do not for the moment believe, this island or a large part of it were subjugated and starving, then our empire beyond the seas, armed and guarded by the British Fleet, will carry on the struggle until in God's good time the

New World with all its power and might, sets forth to the liberation and rescue of the Old."[5]

Basically, he was telling them: <u>Never give up</u>!

Whatever has happened to cause you to be brought low, just remember God heals broken hearts, restores broken dreams, gives beauty for ashes, exchanges sorrows for joy, restores health, and avenges His own, replenishing double! You may have scars, but they are healed scars, touched by the finger of God with pure love.

Your times are in His hands: "My times are in Your hand; deliver me from the hand of my enemies, and from those who persecute me" (Psalm 31:15, NKJV).

The enemy can be any number of things, but all enemies are under subjection to Almighty God. They cannot destroy you or keep you in the pit of failure or discouragement. You were born to fly like an eagle. God keeps His Word, His promises are true, and great is His faithfulness.

Go ahead and look out your window and see what the weather is today; it does not matter whether it's windy, rainy, sunny, or stormy. God's promises are not contingent on the weather. Open your discouraged heart and accept His offer of mercy. He has not abandoned you, you are not alone; you are loved by God and He cares about you. And He is going to perform a work of regeneration in your heart. He says, "Behold I have graven thee upon the palms of my hands" (Isaiah 49:16).

No doubt a part of the wonder which is concentrated in the word *Behold*, is excited by the unbelieving lamentation of the preceding sentence. Zion said, "The LORD hath forsaken me, and my God hath forgotten me." How amazed the divine mind seems to be at this wicked unbelief! What can be more astounding than the unfounded doubts and fears of God's favored people? The Lord's loving word of rebuke should make us blush; He cries, "How can I have forgotten thee, when I have graven thee upon the palms of my hands? How darest thou doubt my constant remembrance, when the memorial is set upon my very flesh?" It does not say, "Thy name." The name is there but that is not all: "I have graven *thee*." See the fullness of this! I have graven thy person, thine image, thy case, thy circumstances, thy sins, thy temptations, thy weaknesses, thy wants, thy works, I have graven *thee*, everything about thee, all that concerns thee; I have put thee altogether there. Wilt thou ever say again that thy God hath forsaken thee when He has graven *thee* upon His own palms?" –SPURGEON[6]

Know that God is with you at all times. He will never leave you nor forsake you. He hears every cry. Every time you call on His name, He is listening. You were not born to fail, but you were born to sit with Him in heavenly places and soar in the realm of the Spirit! "They that wait upon the LORD shall renew their strength; they shall mount up with wings as eagles; they shall run, and not be weary; and they shall walk, and not faint" (Isaiah 40:31).

So go ahead, and let God strengthen your wings; it's time to soar!

EPILOGUE

In summary, Philip Van Doren Stern wrote a story about a man who said, "I wish I had never been born." Later it was made into a film entitled "It's a Wonderful Life." It told what life would have been if he had not been born.

You were born for a reason. Consider the following people in the Bible; they all had moments when they felt like dying before they accomplished the purpose:

- Joseph was sold into slavery and cast into prison for a crime he didn't commit.
- Daniel was thrown into a lions' den.
- Esther feared for her life when she interceded for her people.
- David was chased by a jealous and crazy man.
- Elijah was threatened by a diabolical woman and said, "Let me die."
- Paul was beaten, stoned, and left for dead.

God has a purpose for you. It may look like a trial, but it's a blessing in disguise. The trial has a greater purpose than just you going through a difficulty. You can't go by what is seen on the surface of things.

During the invasion of Scotland after a long siege of one of the castles, the invaders, thinking their foes must be near the point of starvation, sent a message demanding surrender.

In reply, a great string of fresh fish was hung over the wall. A subterranean passage to the sea enabled them to obtain a boundless supply.

So are "the exceeding riches of his grace in his kindness toward us through Christ Jesus" (Ephesians 2:7). –WILBER E. NELSON[1]

From other people's observations, it may appear you are about to surrender and give up, but don't you dare, not when you have God Almighty on your side, cheering you on.

His mercy is forever to all generations. He is there for you at all times, as Psalm 94:18–19 so clearly promises: "When I said, My foot slippeth; thy mercy, O LORD, held me up" (KJV). "When doubts filled my mind, your comfort gave me renewed hope and cheer" (NLT).

No matter what happens to you, there is always hope when you trust in God. He will work His plan out in your life. It's forward all the way!

Segments of his battle line were falling back in disorder and defeat. "Beat a retreat!" shouted Napoleon to a drummer boy. Saluting smartly, the heroic drummer boy said, "Sir, you never taught me to beat a retreat. I can only beat a charge!" The lad's reply kindled new courage in Napoleon, who instantly gave the command, "Then beat a charge, drummer boy!" He did and seeming defeat was turned into victory. The

Captain of our salvation, the Lord Jesus, commands, "Forward!"[2]

Paul wrote: "Brethren, I count not myself to have apprehended: but this one thing I do, forgetting those things which are behind, and reaching forth unto those things which are before" (Philippians 3:13).

The message is loud and clear: There's no retreat, no living in the regrets of the past; it's going forward to victory and the prize.

Abigail Adams wrote to her son, John Quincy Adams, on January 19, 1780, before he became president of the United States of America, the following words: "It is not in the still calm of life, or in the repose of a pacific station that great characters are formed. . . . Great necessities call out great virtues."

You do have the ability to soar, and to go forward through Christ! Show yourself and others that you *can* according to Philippians 4:13: "I can do all things through Christ which strengtheneth me."

Notes

INTRODUCTION

1. Howell, Clinton T., *Lines to Live By* (New York, NY: Thomas Nelson Inc., 1972), 178.
2. Tan, Paul Lee, *Encyclopedia of 7,700 Illustrations* (Rockville, MD: Assurance Publishers, 1979), 1312.

CHAPTER 1

1. Knight, Walter B., *Knight's Treasury of Illustrations* (Grand Rapids, MI: Eerdmans, 1963), 223.
2. https://www.smithsonianmag.com/science-nature/the-story-of-the-most-common-bird-in-the-world-113046500/
3. Tan, 1313.
4. Frank, Leonard Roy, ed., *Random House Webster's Quotationary* (New York: Random House, 1999), 207.
5. Spurgeon, C. H., *Morning and Evening*, (Scotland and Great Britain: Christian Focus Publications, 1994), April 29, Morning.

CHAPTER 2

1. This lyrics to this hymn were written by Katharina A. von Schlegel and translated by Jane L. Borthwick. http://library.timelesstruths.org.

2. Henry, Matthew, *Matthew Henry's Commentary on the Whole Bible*, Vol.III Job to Song of Solomon (New York, London, and Edinburgh: Fleming H. Revell Co., 1710), 236–237.

3. Knight, 4.

4. Knight, 250.

5. As told by W. W. Weeks in Knight, 332.

6. Spurgeon, June 28, Morning.

CHAPTER 3

1. Knight, 370.

2. Martin, Ralph P., Hawthorne, Gerald F., Reid, Daniel G., *Dictionary of Paul and His Letters: A Compendium of Contemporary Biblical Scholarship* (Westmont IL: Intervarsity, 1993).

3. Tan, 1509.

4. Knight, 425.

5. Goodreads.com/MatthewHenry

CHAPTER 4

1. Frank, 513.

2. Goodreads.com/MatthewHenry

3. http://biblehub.com/commentaries/gill/judges/11.htm

4. Cho, Dr. Paul Yonggi, *The Fourth Dimension,* (Plainfield, NJ: Logos International, 1979), 67–68.

CHAPTER 5

1. Frank, 879.
2. Howell, 43.
3. Robinson, Thomas, DD, *Preacher's complete Homiletical Commentary on the Old Testament, Book of Job,* (New York, London, and Toronto: Funk & Wagnalls, 1892), 234.
4. Goodreads.com/MatthewHenry, italics in original.

CHAPTER 6

1. Knight, 298.
2. Knight, 336. https://www.christianitytoday.com/history/people/scholarsandscientists/william-tyndale.html
3. Tan, 1273.
4. Knight, 371.
5. Goodreads.com/MatthewHenry

CHAPTER 7

1. Frank, 210.
2. Hillel (first century BC), rabbinical writings from the Talmud (AD 1st–6th century), quoted in Frank, 576.
3. The material in the chapter up to this point is taken from my book, *The Blessing of the Prison.*
4. Knight, 374.
5. Tan, 1510.
6. Howell, 138.
7. Spurgeon, June 30, Evening.

Chapter 8

1. Howell, 48.
2. Knight, 148.
3. Spurgeon, March 29, Evening.
4. Knight, 173.
5. Goodreads.com/MatthewHenry

Chapter 9

1. Frank, 574.
2. Knight, 148.
3. Howell, 44.
4. Spurgeon, November 4, Morning.

Chapter 10

1. Frank, 839.
2. Frank, 207.
3. Knight, 263.
4. Tan, 1566.
5. Tan, 252–253.
6. Spurgeon, November 7, Morning.

Epilogue

1. Tan, 520.
2. Knight, 81.
3. Frank, 333.

SELECTED BIBLIOGRAPHY

Cho, Paul Yonggi. *The Fourth Dimension*. Plainfield, NJ: Logos International, 1979.

Frank, Leonard Roy, ed. *Random House Webster's Quotationary*. New York: Random House, 1999.

Gill, John. *Gill's Exposition on the Entire Bible*. London, 1746–63; Internet Sacred Text Archive, 2018.

Henry, Matthew. *Complete Commentary on the Whole Bible*. New York, London, and Edinburgh, 1710; Internet Sacred Text Archive, 2018.

Howell, Clinton T. *Lines to Live By*. New York, NY: Thomas Nelson, 1972.

Knight, Walter B. *Knight's Treasury of Illustrations*. Grand Rapids, MI: Eerdmans, 1963.

Martin, Ralph P., Hawthorne, Gerald F., and Reid, Daniel G. *Dictionary of Paul and His Letters: A Compendium of Contemporary Biblical Scholarship*. Westmont IL: Intervarsity, 1993.

Robinson, Thomas, DD. *Preacher's Complete Homiletical Commentary on the Old Testament*. New York, London, and Toronto: Funk & Wagnalls, 1892).

Spurgeon, C. H. *Morning and Evening*. Scotland and Great Britain: Christian Focus Publications, 1994.

Tan, Paul Lee. *Encyclopedia of 7,700 Illustrations.* Rockville, MD: Assurance Publishers, 1979.